MORE

JESUS

MORE

J♥Y

365

Sandy Holly

Learn more about becoming a "Jesus freak"
at **www.JesusFreakApparel.com**

Printed in the United States of America

~Dedication~

For Jesus, my joyful Encourager to whom I owe all my joy.

~Contents~

~*Joy*~

Pronounced: (joi)

Noun: feeling and emotion of pleasure, obtaining what one desires

Synonyms: delight, jubilation, exultation, happiness, bliss, rapture

Joy in the Holy Bible is induced by the Holy Spirit who causes us to see and feel the joy of Jesus in any situation.

Joy is not an emotion that can be forced; it has to be felt, and it is not dependent upon our circumstances.

Joy is felt when we spend time in the presence of Jesus—praising Him; living an honest, biblical life; and recognizing what He has already done for us.

Jesus equals joy.

~Introduction~

Here's the thing about joy: it's everywhere, and it's ours for the taking. We can choose joy, find it, be in it, and live in it whenever we want. No matter what situation we are facing in life, we can find joy in it. John 10:10 states that Jesus came to give us life and to give it to us more abundantly! That's not a ho-hum kind of existence. It's a freedom and extravagant-joy kind of living.

I had an absolute blast writing *More Jesus More Joy 365*. Searching the Bible and my life for acts of joy was such a blessing to me. I didn't want the experience to end, as God handpicked the 365 that He wants to share with you. Through this process I accumulated so much joy that I have it bankrolled and can spend it whenever I want. I want to spend it, live in, love in, and share that joy daily with you. Let's go on a God-filled adventure together as He shows us the joys of His heart.

This journey to discover joy is a 365-day daily devotional to join the believers of Jesus together. Join in the community of joy by posting and following the daily devo hashtags on social media. Each day has an individual daily hashtag for that day's activity. We can find joy in our activity and also find joy in each other's day. Attach the daily hashtag to your post, and you can use upper or lower case letters in the hashtag. I used a mix of both to make it easier to read. Each day will have a new joy for you to explore and express. Your expression can be in any form; share in pictures, words, thoughts, music, poetry, memes, doodles, paints, pens, markers, or any medium that brings your heart joy.

Post your interactive joy expressions daily on social media, so we can all be a part of something bigger than we are. Also, tag us or post on the Jesus Freak Apparel Facebook page @RecoveringSinner, click on the community group,

More Jesus More Joy 365. We can all take joy knowing that Jesus in Heaven will be having a blast watching our answers and expressing our love for Him. He will be watching over our community and guiding us in growing strong and loving one another like He has asked us to do. Let's go discover all of the joys Jesus so freely gives us!

January 1

"Give all your worries and cares to God, for he cares about you." (1 Peter 5:7)

Today, let's make a list of our worries and cares, and cast them onto Him. After we write our list and tell God all about it, let's rip it up and throw it away. That's how we'll make more room for joy. Tomorrow will worry about itself; let's live for today. How many worries did you get to throw away? Joy in worrying less.

#MoreJesusMoreJoy365WorryLess

January 2

"A cheerful look brings joy to the heart; good news makes for good health." (Proverbs 15:30)

Today, let's smile 365 times. Oh, yes, you read that right! Three-hundred and sixty-five times and keep track with pen and paper. Flash those pearly whites at anyone and everyone. Give them the biggest God-filled smile you got; well, 365 of them to be exact. Maybe add a polite head nod to go with that blazing smile. After today, smiling will become your automatic. Boy, is that a joyous attribute! How many smiles can you do? Joy in spreading it.

#MoreJesusMoreJoy365SpreadJoy

January

3

"I have hidden your word in my heart, that I might not sin against you." (Psalm 119:11)

Today, let's scan our Bible to learn a new passage of scripture. After you find a verse that speaks to your heart, write it on paper. Carry it with you, and tape it on your car dash, work station, locker, or bathroom mirror. Leave it there until you have memorized the verse. Recite the scripture every day until it is imprinted on your heart. Joy in hidden words.

#MoreJesusMoreJoy365HiddenWords

January

4

"Blessed are the peacemakers, for they will be called children of God." (Matthew 5:9, NIV)

Today, let's examine our fences and determine if ours need mending. Who or what comes to mind? Make every effort willed by the Holy Spirit to make peace before the sun goes down. Jesus loves those who are peacemakers. Joy in peacemaking.

#MoreJesusMoreJoy365MendingFences

January 5

"For I can do everything through Christ, who gives me strength." (Philippians 4:13)

Today, let's write out our top ten things to accomplish in the next year. You don't need to rank them; just jot them down after much prayerful thought. Then start accomplishing the tasks and cross them off. Maybe frame them and post them someplace where you can see the list daily. It will be so joyful to get your tasks out of your head and onto paper. Tackle the tasks; let nothing stand in your way. Show us your top ten! Joy in His motivation.

#MoreJesusMoreJoy365TopTen

January 6

"I pray that God, the source of hope, will fill you completely with joy and peace because you trust in him. Then you will overflow with confident hope through the power of the Holy Spirit." (Romans 15:13)

Today, let's add a new color of highlighter or pen to outline our Bible readings. When you look back, you'll remember all of the lessons you spent seeking and learning during the year and overflow with joy. What's your new color? Joy in learning.

#MoreJesusMoreJoy365learning

January

7

"And all the people followed Solomon into Jerusalem, playing flutes and shouting for joy. The celebration was so joyous and noisy that the earth shook with the sound." (1 Kings 1:40)

Today, let's listen for the earth to shake with the sound of joy in Sunday church. Can you feel the vibration of the music playing and everyone singing? Clap along and make a joyful noise. Show us a picture of your Sunday service. Joy in celebrating Jesus.

#MoreJesusMoreJoy365SundayService

January

8

"Consequently, faith comes from hearing the message, and the message is heard through the word about Christ." (Romans 10:17, NIV)

Today, let's skip our favorite TV show and spend some time in God's Word. Try it—even if you have already had your quiet time today. This is bonus time with Him. What show did you skip? Joy in growing faith.

#MoreJesusMoreJoy365GrowingFaith

January
9

"Be still, and know that I am God!" (Psalm 46:10)

Today, let's be still with God. Spend one minute meditating on God's words, *"Be still"* Give Him one minute; set a timer if you need to. Relax into Him, allow your mind to think about the verse and what it means to you. Share with us how that minute went. Joy in the stillness of God.

#MoreJesusMoreJoy365BeStill

January
10

"Give thanks to the LORD, for he is good! His faithful love endures forever." (Psalm 106:1)

Today, let's show our love in unexpected gestures of joy. Perhaps, you can go out of your way to hold the door for someone; the person will easily see you noticed him or her. Or take a meal or a treat to a friend's house so that person will see your love and feel joy in the unexpected. Show us your unexpected joy gestures. Joy in unexpected, enduring love for others.

#MoreJesusMoreJoy365UnexpectedJoy

January 11

"But I say, love your enemies! Pray for those who persecute you!" (Matthew 5:44)

Today, let's take time to pray for those who are persecuting you. It's hard to love those who are hard to love, so be mindful and pray open-hearted to God. Find joy in tough times because in your heart you know the end of the story. Blessed are you when you pray for others. Share a warrior prayer for our enemies. Joy in praying for our enemies.

MoreJesusMoreJoy365EnemyPrayers

January 12

"Don't use foul or abusive language. Let everything you say be good and helpful, so that your words will be an encouragement to those who hear them." (Ephesians 4:29)

Today, let's find the positive in every conversation—whether it's with family, friends, coworkers, or employers. Look for glimpses of joy and hang on to them. Promote the joy you're hearing and encourage it by adding to it. Whose conversation do you find the most joyful? Joy in building up each other.

MoreJesusMoreJoy365PositiveWords

January 13

"I will sing to the LORD as long as I live. I will praise my God to my last breath!" (Psalm 104:33)

Today, let's warm up those vocal cords and belt one out to the great I Am. Sing to the Lord on your way to work or while making dinner. Invite your family and friends to join in. It can be as simple as a childhood hymn, and it doesn't matter how good a singer you are or are not. He loves you so much, He can't wait to hear your voice sing His name. Which song did you sing to Him? Joy in praising Him to the last breath.

#MoreJesusMoreJoy365LastBreath

January 14

"I am coming soon. Hold on to what you have, so that no one will take away your crown." (Revelation 3:11)

Today, put on your imaginary crown or real one if you have one. You're royalty! You are the daughter or the son of the King! As royalty, walk the red carpet, it's rolled out for you, all the way to the cross. Hold onto your crown. Show us your crown. Joy in awaiting His return.

MoreJesusMoreJoy365royalty

January

15

"Take my yoke upon you. Let me teach you, because I am humble and gentle at heart, and you will find rest for your souls." (Matthew 11:29)

Today, let's wear our favorite clothes. It doesn't matter if there are holes in them or if they're out of style, put them on and enjoy the comfort. Rest in the comfort of being yoked right alongside of Jesus as you read His Word today and learn from Him. Show us your comfort. Joy in the comfort of Jesus.

#MoreJesusMoreJoy365comfort

January

16

"Keep putting into practice all you learned and received from me—everything you heard from me and saw me doing. Then the God of peace will be with you." (Philippians 4:9)

Today, let's search our minds in prayer to find a truth from God to practice. What is God asking you to work on? Is it self-discipline, diet and exercise, or reading the Bible daily? Joy in practice.

#MoreJesusMoreJoy365practice

January

17

"When times are good, be happy; but when times are bad, consider this: God has made the one as well as the other." (Ecclesiastes 7:14, NIV)

Today, let's write out a note that states "God is in control." Whatever trial we may be going through, we can choose to see the joy in it. Reverence to God allows us to choose joy in our trials and to understand that they too only last for a time—as difficult as they may be. We can choose joy because we still have the promise of Jesus. How do you choose joy in bad times? Joy in choosing it.

#MoreJesusMoreJoy365choosingJoy

January

18

"The eyes of the LORD watch over those who do right; his ears are open to their cries for help." (Psalm 34:15)

Today, let's pull down God's great big ear and whisper our cries to Him. Take time and tell Him all about it. He can't wait to hear from you. He is always ready to hear the cries and praises of the ones who love Him. What does it look like to pull down God's ear? Joy in being heard.

#MoreJesusMoreJoy365heard

January

19

"And now, dear brothers and sisters, one final thing. Fix your thoughts on what is true, and honorable, and right, and pure, and lovely, and admirable. Think about things that are excellent and worthy of praise." (Philippians 4:8)

Today, let's be mindful of what we're watching on TV, the music to which we're listening, the magazines or books we're reading, and the conversations we're having. Whatever goes into our minds comes out in our thoughts or actions. Let's fix our minds on something lovely. What's your lovely? Joy in a pure mind.

#MoreJesusMoreJoy365PureMind

January

20

"God is within her, she will not fall; God will help her at break of day." (Psalm 46:5, NIV)

Today, let's look back at a time we have fallen down. Where was it at, and did you run ahead of God? Was He even invited to your adventure? When we run ahead of God, we will almost always fall. When we remain in God, He will be with us, and we will not fall. Joy in remaining faithful to God.

#MoreJesusMoreJoy365faithful

January 21

"I have told you these things so that you will be filled with my joy. Yes, your joy will overflow!"
(John 15:11)

Today, let's examine joy and how we attain and keep it. Joy is spiritual, a product from our time spent with Jesus. We attain joy through the knowledge of the Bible. When life's trials come our way, we remain levelheaded because of our time spent with Jesus and the joy we've cultivated in Him. Does your joy overflow or do you need more time with Him? Joy in spending time with Jesus.

#MoreJesusMoreJoy365TimeWithJesus

January 22

"Worry weighs a person down; an encouraging word cheers a person up." (Proverbs 12:25)

Today, let's be the joy we want to see in the world and propel each other forward. Let's send something uplifting to ten people by text, message, or a note. Prayerfully consider your words and then share them. Also share them with us! Joy in an encouraging word.

#MoreJesusMoreJoy365EncouragingWord

January

23

"Understand this, my dear brothers and sisters:
You must all be quick to listen, slow to speak,
and slow to get angry." (James 1:19)

Today, let's practice using our beautiful, God-given ears and listen intently to others without formulating our response. Ingest the conversation from them, spend a second waiting for God's response, then you get to talk. This is sometimes hard to do, especially when we are passionate about something. How well did you listen? Joy in really listening.

#MoreJesusMoreJoy365listening

January

24

"You saw me before I was born. Every day of my life was recorded in your book. Every moment was laid out before a single day had passed." (Psalm 139:16)

Today, let's write down this truth of scripture and carry it with us. Share it with someone you know is expecting or be on the lookout for women who are expecting. Take notice of their God-given glow as He has created life yet again. Share with them this truth, and let your joy become their new joy. Joy in His recorded days.

#MoreJesusMoreJoy365RecordedDays

January

25

"Be joyful in hope, patient in affliction, faithful in prayer." (Romans 12:12, NIV)

Today, let's be faithful in prayer. The next time someone mentions in passing that someone needs prayer, or he needs prayer, stop right then, and pray for and with them. Stay faithful in prayer and be sure to take it a step further and keep a pocket prayer journal. Take your time in prayer and petition God on another's behalf. Ask Him to intervene with help. Show us how you keep track of prayers. Joy in faithful prayer.

#MoreJesusMoreJoy365FaithfulPrayer

January

26

"Study this Book of Instruction continually. Meditate on it day and night so you will be sure to obey everything written in it. Only then will you prosper and succeed in all you do." (Joshua 1:8)

Today, let's recommit ourselves to the obedience of reading God's Word. Let's weed out some of the distractions in our day and meditate on His Word day and night until it becomes our new normal. When is the best time for you to read and meditate on His Word? Joy in reading the Bible.

#MoreJesusMoreJoy365ReadTheBible

January

27

"So you have sorrow now, but I will see you again; then you will rejoice, and no one can rob you of that joy." (John 16:22)

Today, let's be reminded that nobody can rob our joy. We get to live in joy whenever we want, and no one can ever rob us of that joy. What makes you so joyful that no one could possibly take it from you? Is it a vision of heaven you keep on a loop in your mind or is it the daily lessons you get from Jesus as you read the Bible? No one can rob your joy because no one can take your knowledge of Jesus. Joy in keeping it.

#MoreJesusMoreJoy365KeepingJoy

January

28

"Come, everyone! Clap your hands! Shout to God with joyful praise!" (Psalm 47:1)

Today, let's overflow with joy and look for the last three moments of joy you've experienced. Was it as simple as the smell of a fresh brewed cup of coffee or as complex as a roof over your head? Record your joys and shout and share them with us! Joy in every God-given thing.

#MoreJesusMoreJoy365ShoutsOfJoy

January

29

"She is clothed with strength and dignity; she can laugh at the days to come." (Proverbs 31:25, NIV)

Today, let's practice laughing out loud. Think of a funny joke and tell it to someone everywhere you go. You are a child of God, and He has taken away your worries. We are all confident with who we are in Him. We can laugh today and for the days to come. Tell us your funny joke. Joy in sharing laughter.

#MoreJesusMoreJoy365ShareLaughter

January

30

"I am leaving you with a gift—peace of mind and heart. And the peace I give is a gift the world cannot give. So don't be troubled or afraid." (John 14:27)

Today, let's rest in Jesus' peace and tell Him all about our troubled hearts. Jesus reminds us that the peace He gives us surpasses what the world offers. Finding peace amongst the chaos is finding Jesus. Share what God's peace looks like to you. Joy in God's peace.

#MoreJesusMore365GodsPeace

January

31

"Jesus told him, 'I am the way, the truth, and the life. No one can come to the Father except through me.'" (John 14:6)

Today, let's direct traffic and have all our signs point to Jesus. You've seen some signs like "Jesus at work," "One way— Jesus," and "Jesus Saves." Maybe your town has one or in your travels, you snapped a fun picture of a Jesus traffic sign. There are so many roads, detours, and choices but only One Way; that's Jesus. Let's encourage the flow of traffic to follow Jesus for His is the Way, and He is the One to follow. Joy in a one-way ticket.

#MoreJesusMoreJoy365TheWay

February

1

"But anyone who does not love does not know God, for God is love." (1 John 4:8)

Today, let's make known that God is love by our actions. If we are in Him, we are called to love everyone—even those who are hard to love. No excuses are acceptable. Do you love like Him? Share a picture or a thought of what God's love looks like to you. Joy in loving everyone.

#MoreJesusMoreJoy365GodIsLove

February

2

"Most important of all, continue to show deep love for each other, for love covers a multitude of sins." (1 Peter 4:8)

Today, let's examine our lives and determine if we are withholding love from someone. Maybe it's a distant family member or a co-worker. Maybe it's your spouse. Who do you need to love deeply? Get into that nook of your life, pray over it and ask God to speak into it. Ask God to show you how to love through it. Joy in loving deeply.

#MoreJesusMoreJoy365DeepLove

February

3

"Above all, clothe yourselves with love, which binds us all together in perfect harmony." (Colossians 3:14)

Today, let's consider what it looks like to be clothed in love like Jesus and living life in harmony. Of all the virtues and emotions we have, the last one that we put on is love, which binds it all together. What does it look like to be clothed in love? Is it peaceful? Does it have a color? Joy clothed in love.

#MoreJesusMoreJoy365ClothedInLove

February

4

"So now I am giving you a new commandment: Love each other. Just as I have loved you, you should love each other. Your love for one another will prove to the world that you are my disciples." (John 13:34, 35)

Today, let's tell of a time, a place, or a person in your life where love was easily seen. You know the kind of person; before even speaking with him, clearly Jesus was in this place. God's modern-day disciples are easy to see because of how they love. They are quick to listen, slow to speak, and usually ready to flash a smile because of the joy in their heart. Joy as a disciple of Jesus.

#MoreJesusMoreJoy365DiscipleOfJesus

February

5

"And the very hairs on your head are all numbered." (Matthew 10:30)

Today, let's go for a haircut. If you've been recently, at your next appointment, ask your stylist or barber if he or she knew that every one of their hairs on their head are numbered and known by God. Ask the person how many "numbers" he or she swept up in a day's work? Or share and tag a stylist in this scripture. Joy in being known completely by God.

#MoreJesusMoreJoy365IAmKnown

February

6

"He acted with a strong hand and powerful arm. His faithful love endures forever." (Psalm 136:12)

Today, let's continue to celebrate His great love for us and think of someone to whom you can extend your arm. Ask God to place a person or a place on your heart, obey him and check in with them. Ask how you can be of service to them. Extend the powerful arm He gave to help others. Who did He place on your heart? Joy in helping others.

#MoreJesusMoreJoy365HelpOthers

February

7

"For he will order his angels to protect you wherever you go." (Psalm 91: 11)

Today, let's be reminded that we are protected by His angels. Put on an angel pin or a piece of jewelry, a pocket token, or simply draw a halo on your hand. Take comfort in the reminder that you're protected as a follower of Jesus. He has sent angels to watch over and protect you. Show your angels. Joy in the care of angels.

#MoreJesusMoreJoy365AngelProtection

February

8

"And the Holy Spirit helps us in our weakness. For example, we don't know what God wants us to pray for. But the Holy Spirit prays for us with groanings that cannot be expressed in words." (Romans 8:26)

Today, let's present ourselves before the Lord with just a simple smile on our face. We can reveal our hearts and minds to the Holy Spirit who will pray on our behalf. It doesn't get any better than that! God cares for us even when we cannot express ourselves with words. Did you have peace praying with no words? Joy in being speechless.

#MoreJesusMoreJoy365speechless

February

9

"For we know how dearly God loves us, because he has given us the Holy Spirit to fill our hearts with his love." (Romans 5:5)

Today, let's embrace the Holy Spirit as yet another gift from God. We can call on the Holy Spirit when alone, sad, or happy. How has the Holy Spirit filled your heart with love? Invite the Spirit to hold you. Joy in a holy hug.

#MoreJesusMoreJoy365HolyHug

February 10

"Love is patient and kind. Love is not jealous or boastful or proud or rude. It does not demand its own way. It is not irritable, and it keeps no record of being wronged." (1 Corinthians 13:4, 5)

Today, let's spend some time thinking about someone who has wronged us. Take time and write out the things they've done wrong to you. Then before God, decide to cancel their debt and throw away the paper. God doesn't keep track of wrongs, and neither should we. Show us your shreds of paper. There's so much freedom in not keeping score. Joy in what love is.

#MoreJesusMoreJoy365WhatLoveIs

February 11

"You are altogether beautiful, my darling, beautiful in every way." (Songs 4:7)

Today, let's share this truth with someone dear in your life. This will put a spring in the person's step and also yours. This is how God sees you—so precious and beautiful. Can't you just hear Him calling you *darling*? With whom will you share this? Joy in being loved.

#MoreJesusMoreJoy365KingdomBeautiful

February

12

"Jesus replied, 'You must love the LORD your God with all your heart, all your soul, and all your mind.'" (Matthew 22:37)

Today, let's keep God on our hearts, souls, and minds and doodle His name on anything and everything. Create your Jesus art on a long conference call. While waiting to pick up your kids, grab your journal. Show us your creations. Joy in having Jesus on the mind.

#MoreJesusMoreJoy365HeartSoulMind

February

13

"Take delight in the LORD, and he will give you your heart's desires." (Psalm 37:4)

Today, let's boldly ask God to give us the desires of our heart. What does your heart desire? Spend today considering and confirming exactly what your heart desires. Then bring it before the Lord. Bow down, give him your heart in prayer and simply ask. Joy in recognition of your heart's desire.

#MoreJesusMoreJoy365HeartsDesire

February 14

"I have found the one whom my heart loves."
(Songs 3:4, emphasis mine)

Today, let's use scripture and write a love note to a loved one. Short on loved ones? God is always eager to hear from us. Song of Songs is full of beautiful, imagery-expressing love. Which verse or verses did you use? Joy in expressing love.

#MoreJesusMoreJoy365ExpressLove

February 15

"The Spirit and the bride say, 'Come!' And let the one who hears say, 'Come!' Let the one who is thirsty come; and let the one who wishes take the free gift of the water of life." (Revelation 22:17, NIV)

Today, let's be reminded of the free gift of life that we are given through Jesus. Wrap up a small, empty gift box, and place it somewhere to be reminded that today is a gift. Or tie some ribbons and bows on a bottle of water to remember that He is the water of life. Today is a gift; you won't have it tomorrow, so open up the gift of life today. Joy in accepting Jesus.

#MoreJesusMoreJoy365TodayIsAGift

February

16

"Because your love is better than life, my lips will glorify you." (Psalm 63:3, NIV)

Today, let your lips glorify God and say a prayer out loud to Him. Pray something like this: "You are so good, God. There is no one like You, and Your love lasts forever and ever. Amen" Share your prayer praise with us. Joy in praising Him out loud.

#MoreJesusMoreJoy365OutLoudPraise

February

17

"Instead, be kind to each other, tenderhearted, forgiving one another, just as God through Christ has forgiven you." (Ephesians 4:32)

Today, let's think of someone who needs our forgiveness and make the decision to forgive. Send a text, a note, or a call to start the healing process. Be patient and, above all, display compassion in your forgiveness. Let them know you were thinking about them and want to make things right again. What are some other ways to start the conversation? Since God forgave us, we can forgive others. Joy in forgiveness.

#MoreJesusMoreJoy365forgiveness

February 18

"And I am certain that God, who began the good work within you, will continue his work until it is finally finished on the day when Christ Jesus returns." (Philippians 1:6)

Today, let's make ourselves a little sign that states "I am a work in progress" Hang it someplace prominent to be reminded that He will carry you through to completion. Show us your sign. Joy in being a work in progress.

#MoreJesusMoreJoy365unfinished

February 19

"Jesus Christ is the same yesterday, today, and forever." (Hebrews 13:8)

Today, let's remember someone or something that we will love forever. Of course, it's Jesus, but what else will you love forever? Is it a parent, a spouse, a pet? Forever isn't timed, and joy is limitless. Who's your forever love? Joy in forever loving like Jesus.

#MoreJesusMoreJoy365LoveLikeJesus

February

20

"I lie awake thinking of you, meditating on you through the night." (Psalm 63:6)

Today, let's think about what you want to tell God tonight before you fall asleep. Tonight as your head hits the pillow, tell Him all about your day—every last detail. He's been waiting all day to hear from you. What will you tell Him? Joy in the day's reflection.

#MoreJesusMoreJoy365DaysReflection

February

21

"Therefore, God elevated him to the place of highest honor and gave him the name above all other names." (Philippians 2:9)

Today, let's look at our first name and our surname. If you can, call or text your parents and thank them for naming you. If your parents have passed, write them a letter expressing your gratitude for them. Your name is joyous, but there is no greater name than Jesus. How'd you get your name? Joy in the name above all names.

#MoreJesusMoreJoy365NoGreaterName

February

22

"For you are all children of the light and of the day; we don't belong to darkness and night." (1 Thessalonians 5:5)

Today, let's rejoice in the truth, and every time you switch on a light, repeat the following: *"I am one of the children of the light"* How many lights did you turn on? Rejoice as we are children of the light in the light of day—no longer belonging to darkness. Joy as children of the light.

#MoreJesusMoreJoy365ChildrenOfLight

February

23

"How wonderful to be wise, to analyze and interpret things. Wisdom lights up a person's face, softening its harshness." (Ecclesiastes 8:1)

Today, let's flip open the Bible and read a few verses. Let's get in the habit of getting God's perspective and reap the benefit of a Godly glow. Wisdom comes from knowing and spending time in God's Word. What did you analyze, and what wisdom did you gain today? Joy in wisdom.

#MoreJesusMoreJoy365wisdom

February 24

"Accept my prayer as incense offered to you, and my upraised hands as an evening offering."
(Psalm 141:2)

Today, let's light a candle and have a chat with the Lord. Our prayers are a pleasing aroma to Him. Let the glorious scent fill the room and your heart. What scent did you burn? Joy in the sense of smell.

#MoreJesusMoreJoy365ScentedPrayer

February 25

"Then Jesus said, 'Whoever has ears to hear, let them hear.'" (Mark 4:9, NIV)

Today, let's stop singing and close our eyes at church during worship service. Focus only on your ears and what they are hearing. Sounds of both young and old, the crying of babies—take it all in. What did your ears hear? Hold that gratitude in your heart as a gift from God. Joy in praising God with your ears.

#MoreJesusMoreJoy365EarsToHear

February

26

"Though one may be overpowered, two can defend themselves. A cord of three strands is not quickly broken." (Ecclesiastes 4:12, NIV)

Today, let's create joy in written appreciation. Think of a relationship that God has placed in your life—maybe your spouse or a close friend. Write the person a quick text or a note that reminds him or her how God has brought you two together. God is the first strand in the cord. Who's in your cord? Joy in God-derived relationships.

#MoreJesusMoreJoy365ThreeStrands

February

27

"Praise his name with dancing, accompanied by tambourine and harp." (Psalm 149:3)

Today, let's try *kitchen dancing*. Let your Jesus Freak flag fly in your kitchen as you dance, sing and praise His holy name for an entire worship song. If you're having fun, and I know you will be, try two songs! Even better...try not counting the songs and dance away. To what song did you dance? Joy in dancing before God.

#MoreJesusMoreJoy365PraiseHisName

February

28

"In the same way, let your light shine before others, that they may see your good deeds and glorify your Father in heaven." (Matthew 5:16, NIV)

Today, be mindful of a fellow believer who has impacted you or you have seen make a difference in someone else. Give them a personal phone call to let them know you see how they're working and how they're admired. Thank them for their service. Then praise God for them. Whom do you admire? Joy in admiration.

#MoreJesusMoreJoy365admiration

March

1

"If you claim to be religious but don't control your tongue, you are fooling yourself, and your religion is worthless." (James 1:26)

Today, let's really live out our lives as a reflection of our religion. Strive to keep a tight rein on your lips. Apply a lip balm throughout the day as a reminder to keep a tight rein on your lips. Be mindful of your words, and how they affect others. Are they life-giving and designed to lift others, or are they slanderous-gossip? Joy in honoring God with our speech.

#MoreJesusMoreJoy365speech

March

2

"You must not mistreat or oppress foreigners in any way. Remember, you yourselves were once foreigners in the land of Egypt." (Exodus 22:21)

Today, let's learn a stranger's name. Yep, that's right; we are going to talk to strangers because as adults we're finally allowed to. You'll start just like this: "Hi! My name is _____. What's yours? How's your day going?" Possibly extend a hand to shake if it's welcomed. Listen to the person's response. If it's the standard, "I'm fine; thanks, and you?" simply let them know you saw them and wanted to say hello. Add, "Take care, and have a great rest of your day!" Joy in noticing others.

#MoreJesusMoreJoy365seen

March

3

"Trust in the LORD with all your heart; do not depend on your own understanding." (Proverbs 3:5)

Today, let's follow after Jesus' heart. We believers follow Jesus' heart not our own. Where is He leading you? In what way is He asking you to trust in Him? Joy in following the heart of Jesus.

#MoreJesusMoreJoy365FollowHisHeart

March 4

"Therefore, put on every piece of God's armor so you will be able to resist the enemy in the time of evil. Then after the battle you will still be standing firm." (Ephesians 6:13)

Today, let's envision putting on the armor of God. Place the belt of truth around your waist, adorn yourself with the breastplate of righteousness, firmly plant your feet in peace, and take up the shield to extinguish the flaming arrows from the Enemy. Finally, put on the helmet of salvation and hold the Sword of the Spirit, which is the Holy Bible. What does the armor of God look like to you? Joy in God's armor.

#MoreJesusMoreJoy365ArmorOfGod

March 5

"I will praise you as long as I live, lifting up my hands to you in prayer." (Psalm 63:4)

Today, let's pray to Jesus by lifting up our hands. Pause throughout your day and lift up your hands to Him. Praise Him with a wave and a prayer. Show us your hands of praise! Joy in lifted hands.

#MoreJesusMoreJoy365LiftedHands

March

6

"God blesses those who patiently endure testing and temptation. Afterward they will receive the crown of life that God has promised to those who love him." (James 1:12)

Today, let's ponder the trials we have walked through with God and how He cared for us. As you reflect, keep the vision of Heaven in your heart and imagine the day you will receive your crown. What will your crown look like when He gives it to you? Joy in life's trials.

#MoreJesusMoreJoy365LifeTrials

March

7

"As iron sharpens iron, so a friend sharpens a friend." (Proverbs 27:17)

Today, let's think of a friend who you can encourage and build up. A friend who sharpens a friend is one who intently listens and finds ways to encourage the other's strengths. Pray for your "sharpened" friend. Drop the person a line to let him or her know you're praying and encourage him or her to be the very best. How many sharpened friends do you have? Bringing joy to others, brings joy to yourself. Joy in friendship.

#MoreJesusMoreJoy365SharpenedFriend

March

8

"Don't copy the behavior and customs of this world, but let God transform you into a new person by changing the way you think. Then you will learn to know God's will for you, which is good and pleasing and perfect." (Romans 12:2)

Today, let's consider which ways we are conforming to the customs of this world and which ways we are not. Which of our ways is in the danger zone of conforming? Is it watching questionable television shows or movies? Or has our language, slang, and thought process conformed to the world's norms? Which ways are we allowing God to transform us into a new person? Joy in not conforming to this world.

#MoreJesusMoreJoy365NotConforming

March

9

"God's way is perfect. All the LORD's promises prove true. He is a shield for all who look to him for protection." (Psalm 18:30)

Today, let's pull out our Bibles and highlight this verse in Psalms, which points out that God is perfect and flawless; we can always come to Him. Show us your highlighted scripture. Joy in reverence.

#MoreJesusMoreJoy365reverence

March 10

"In his grace, God has given us different gifts for doing certain things well. So if God has given you the ability to prophesy, speak out with as much faith as God has given you. If your gift is serving others, serve them well. If you are a teacher, teach well." (Romans 12:6, 7)

Today, let's declare the gifts God has given us. Can you paint, write, build, sculpt, organize, lead, educate, or care for others? How do you use your gifts in the workplace and in the home? Joy in using His gifts.

#MoreJesusMoreJoy365HisGifts

March 11

"I press on to reach the end of the race and receive the heavenly prize for which God, through Christ Jesus, is calling us." (Philippians 3:14)

Today, let's hold a sign that declares "Press On!" Use your sign to encourage one another to *press on,* to keep going toward the prize, the prize of Heaven. Show us your signs. Joy in determination.

#MoreJesusMoreJoy365determination

March

12

"Always thanking the Father. He has enabled you to share in the inheritance that belongs to his people, who live in the light." (Colossians 1:12)

Today, let's unite as the people of the light and shine it for all to see! Spread it across social media, thanking the Father for being made part of the kingdom of light. What's your message of light as the light? Joy in the light.

#MoreJesusMoreJoy365TheLight

March

13

"Whatever is good and perfect is a gift coming down to us from God our Father, who created all the lights in the heavens. He never changes or casts a shifting shadow." (James 1:17)

Today, let's fast in reverse. Think about whatever you would normally give up for a fast, and instead, embrace it in abundance. Enjoy it like it's a gift from the Lord to you. Think about how sweet that chocolate will taste when He gives it to you. Or consider the fun binging on social media with Him alongside of you. Joy in His gifts.

#MoreJesusMoreJoy365FastInReverse

March

14

"Yes, I am the vine; you are the branches. Those who remain in me, and I in them, will produce much fruit. For apart from me you can do nothing." (John 15:5)

Today, let's examine our roots, branches, and fruit. When we read the Bible daily and make time for Jesus, we create still deeper roots in Him, which allows us to produce much fruit. How far have your roots extended into the ground? Are you producing fruit? We need Jesus to grow. Joy in growing in the Vine.

#MoreJesusMoreJoy365TheVine

March

15

"Those who say they live in God should live their lives as Jesus did." (1 John 2:6)

Today, let's be reminded to follow His teachings and live as He commanded. As we strive to know more about God, we also strive to be more like Him. Let's try to be more like Jesus, to live and love like Him, and to serve others like Him. How are you trying to be like Jesus? Joy in living your life as Jesus did.

#MoreJesusMoreJoy365LiveLikeJesus

March

16

"If you openly declare that Jesus is Lord and believe in your heart that God raised him from the dead, you will be saved. For it is by believing in your heart that you are made right with God, and it is by openly declaring your faith that you are saved." (Romans 10:9, 10)

Today, let's proclaim our faith in God and invite others to share in God's goodness. Let's recite, repost, and pray out loud this prayer. When did you first pray this prayer? Joy in affirmation.

#MoreJesusMoreJoy365affirmation

March

17

"The people shouted, 'Hosanna!' and declared 'Blessed is he who comes in the name of the Lord.'" (John 12:13, emphasis mine)

Today, let's shout "Hosanna"! This means *save us.* Shout it online, on your way to work, or make it your ringtone. We need reminding of the fact that we need our Savior every day. God save us. Joy in being saved.

#MoreJesusMoreJoy365saved

March

18

"To those who use well what they are given, even more will be given, and they will have an abundance. But from those who do nothing, even what little they have will be taken away." (Matthew 25:29)

Today, let's look around at all of our stuff to see what we have an extra one of. Whatever you find, send it or give it to someone. Maybe it's a couple of extra canned goods; donate them to a local pantry. Why not give that piece of jewelry that you like but no longer wear to a woman's shelter. Send that slightly used pair of work boots or sneakers to the thrift store. What will you re-gift? Or maybe it's a prayer for your local community resource centers. Joy in sharing His abundance.

#MoreJesusMoreJoy365abundance

March

19

"This is the day the LORD has made. We will rejoice and be glad in it." (Psalm 118:24)

Today, let's plan and get ready to have a big belly laugh. You know the kind that you can hardly breathe at first, and then you explode into uncontrolled laughter. Do you get a big belly laugh out of funny videos either on TV or online? Laughter is contagious; try it with a friend. Share a joke or a funny video. Joy in laughter-filled days that He created.

#MoreJesusMoreJoy365laugh

March
20

"Each time he said, 'My grace is all you need. My power works best in weakness.' So now I am glad to boast about my weaknesses, so that the power of Christ can work through me." (2 Corinthians 12:9)

Today, let's search ourselves for our weaknesses and invite God into them. Through God's Word, He whispers, *"My grace is more than enough."* How has God strengthened your weaknesses? Rely on God's grace to strengthen you. Joy in His power.

#MoreJesusMoreJoy365power

March
21

"Jesus spoke to the people once more and said, 'I am the light of the world. If you follow me, you won't have to walk in darkness, because you will have the light that leads to life.'" (John 8:12)

Today, let's share the date we walked into the Light. Maybe it was years ago, or maybe it's today. Let's share the light with a date stamp. Praise God for showing us the light and leading us out of the darkness. Joy in the Light of the world.

#MoreJesusMoreJoy365LightOfLife

March 22

"Think of all the hostility he endured from sinful people; then you won't become weary and give up." (Hebrews 12:3)

Today, let's be reminded not to lose heart and give up. Our days can be hard, but remember, the times when we suffer are the times when God is shaping us the most. Don't lose heart; your victory in Jesus is coming. Let's draw a heart on something and carry it all day. Don't lose your heart. Joy in keeping heart.

#MoreJesusMoreJoy365KeepingHeart

March 23

"He alone is my rock and my salvation, my fortress where I will not be shaken." (Psalm 62:6)

Today, let's declare this psalm and claim it as our anthem. When we have Jesus, we will not be shaken. If we really believe in the truth of Jesus and He alone is our salvation, then don't let this life shake you. Let Psalm 62:6 come to life, as the believers of Jesus Christ will not be shaken. Show us your anthem. Joy in the rock of our salvation.

#MoreJesusMoreJoy365psalm626anthem

March

24

"But you are not like that, for you are a chosen people. You are royal priests, a holy nation, God's very own possession. As a result, you can show others the goodness of God, for he called you out of the darkness into his wonderful light." (1 Peter 2:9)

Today, let's roll out the red carpet for each other with our words and actions. Go the extra mile. Make others feel special and royal. Let's look through Jesus' lenses and love others like He loves. Being reminded how Jesus loves everyone and leads us out of the dark and into the light should be enough motivation to love like Him. How can we make others feel like royalty? Joy in showing others God's goodness.

#MoreJesusMoreJoy365GodsGoodness

March

25

"I will shout for joy and sing your praises, for you have ransomed me." (Psalm 71:23)

Today, let's boldly declare this truth and joy in our lives. We have been ransomed by Jesus, and the ransom He paid has changed our lives forever. Let's record a video declaring this truth by stating this psalm. Joy in being ransomed.

#MoreJesusMoreJoy365ransomed

March

26

"See, I have written your name on the palms of my hands. Always in my mind is a picture of Jerusalem's walls in ruins." (Isaiah 49:16)

Today, let's write Jesus' name on our hands as a reminder that He has our names written on the palms of His hands. Jesus has many names. Choose your favorite: Savior, Good Shepherd, Bright and Morning Star, Immanuel, Messiah, and Lord of Lords—to name only a few. Show us His name on your hand. Joy in the security of His holy name.

#MoreJesusMoreJoy365HisHolyName

March

27

"Since you have been raised to new life with Christ, set your sights on the realities of heaven, where Christ sits in the place of honor at God's right hand." (Colossians 3:2)

Today, let's envision Heaven. Create a vision of Heaven in your heart and visit it often as a reminder this life is only temporary. Heaven is eternal. Share your vision in a picture, in words, in a painting, in poetry, or however you like. Joy in the vision of Heaven.

#MoreJesusMoreJoy365heaven

March

28

"Then Mary took a twelve-ounce jar of expensive perfume made from essence of nard, and she anointed Jesus' feet with it, wiping his feet with her hair. The house was filled with the fragrance." (John 12:3)

Today, let's purposely put on our good perfume or cologne. When the sweet fragrance touches your body, be reminded of the joy and honor Jesus felt as He was anointed by Mary. What's your scent? Joy in His anointing.

#MoreJesusMoreJoy365RememberingJesus

March

29

"Before the Passover celebration, Jesus knew that his hour had come to leave this world and return to his Father. He had loved his disciples during his ministry on earth, and now he loved them to the very end." (John 13:1).

Today, let's consider the great love Jesus had for His disciples and for us today to the end. Let's proclaim this simple truth: "Jesus loves me. The end!" Jesus loved those with whom He walked the earth, and He loves us today—to the very end. Joy in His steadfast love.

#MoreJesusMoreJoy365TheEnd

March

30

"But he was pierced for our transgressions, he was crushed for our iniquities; the punishment that brought us peace was on him, and by his wounds we are healed." (Isaiah 53:5, NIV)

Today, let's remember what Jesus did for us on the cross. The cross was where God drew the line in the sand on the battlefield of salvation. *Come over to the Cross and be saved.* At the cross, Jesus took on all sin, and evil lost all power over those who believed in Him. Do you wear the cross? Joy in the recognition of the cross.

#MoreJesusMoreJoy365TheCross

March

31

"My old self has been crucified with Christ. It is no longer I who live, but Christ lives in me. So I live in this earthly body by trusting in the Son of God, who loved me and gave himself for me." (Galatians 2:20)

Today, let's grab a pen and draw a cross somewhere on our body. Don't wash it off; let it fade away as a reminder that Jesus lives in our heart. Show us your cross. Joy in living for Jesus.

#MoreJesusMoreJoy365LivingForJesus

April 1

"He took some bread and gave thanks to God for it. Then he broke it in pieces and gave it to the disciples, saying, 'This is my body, which is given for you. Do this in remembrance of me.'"
(Luke 22:19)

Today, let's revisit the communion Jesus gave at the Last Supper. Jesus asked His disciples to continue to do this to remember Him. Over 2000 years later, the believers of Jesus still practice taking the Lord's Supper to reflect and remember Him—just as He asked. We eat the bread as a symbol of His body and drink the juice as a symbol of His shed blood. When is the last time you remembered Jesus this way, and how did your thoughts make you feel? Joy in remembering Him.

#MoreJesusMoreJoy365RememberHim

April 2

"Faith shows the reality of what we hope for; it is the evidence of things we cannot see."
(Hebrews 11:1)

Today, let's display our confidence in Jesus. Let's write out the characteristics of who He is. Write out what you personally know about Him. For instance, He is strong, courageous, forgiving. Even though we can't see Him, we still believe in Him. Show us your evidence of faith. Joy in having faith in Jesus.

#MoreJesusMoreJoy365evidence

April

3

"For all who are led by the Spirit of God are children of God." (Romans 8:14)

Today, let's quietly and humbly go before Jesus in prayer. Ask to be filled and led by the Holy Spirit not only today but every day. Through the Spirit, we are adopted by God. Declare your birthright and a name that suits you. You might want to consider one of the following: *adopted, child of God, recovering sinner, adopted by Christ,* or *saved by grace.* Joy in having a Heavenly Father.

#MoreJesusMoreJoy365adopted

April

4

"In every place of worship, I want men to pray with holy hands lifted up to God, free from anger and controversy." (1 Timothy 2:8)

Today, let's go all out to make peace in a place in our life where there is none. It's difficult to communicate with God when unsettled business gets in our way. In prayer, consider your peace-making options so that you can come to God with a clear heart. When you do lift up those hands high, be full of joy! What are some peace-making options? Joy in lifting holy hands.   #MoreJesusMoreJoy365LiftingHands

April 5

"All praise to God, the Father of our Lord Jesus Christ. It is by his great mercy that we have been born again, because God raised Jesus Christ from the dead. Now we live with great expectation." (1 Peter 1:3)

Today, let's be reminded of God's great mercy that He has shown us. Write *mercy* on something and post it in a prominent place. Mercy is forgiveness from the One who has the power to punish us. Show us your mercy and praise Him. Joy in His mercy.

#MoreJesusMoreJoy365HisMercy

April 6

"Isaiah had spoken of John when he said, 'He is a voice shouting in the wilderness, 'Prepare the way for the LORD's coming! Clear the road for him!'" (Luke 3:4)

Today, let's make room for Jesus in our busy lives. To *prepare the way* means "to get rid of our emotional baggage so the Lord has a place to dwell." When we confess our sins and doubts to Him, we are freed from them and space is made for Him. Will you make space for Jesus today? What will you clear away to do so? Joy in clearing the way.

#MoreJesusMoreJoy365ClearTheWay

April
7

"Pray in the Spirit at all times and on every occasion. Stay alert and be persistent in your prayers for all believers everywhere." (Ephesians 6:18)

Today, let's be mindful to continue to pray for others. Do you have a special chair or location where you enjoy praying? If not, determine where yours will be today and ask Jesus to join you. I feel sure He will show up before you even get there! Show us your prayer place. Joy in persistent prayer.

#MoreJesusMoreJoy365PersistentPrayer

April
8

"For the grace of God has been revealed, bringing salvation to all people." (Titus 2:11)

Today, go ahead, reach back and give yourself a pat on the back for accepting His grace! Of all the things we've said yes to in this life, isn't this the most joyful? Show how joyful you are for His grace and pat yourself on the back. Joy in the gift of His grace.

#MoreJesusMoreJoy365grace

April 9

"So Christ has truly set us free. Now make sure that you stay free, and don't get tied up again in slavery to the law." (Galatians 5:1)

Today, let's fly some freedom flags. Jesus has set you free, so see to it that you stay free. The world cannot give this kind of freedom. Share your *"I-am-free"* signs. Joy in God-given freedom.

#MoreJesusMoreJoy365IAmFree

April 10

"Don't forget to show hospitality to strangers, for some who have done this have entertained angels without realizing it!" (Hebrews 13:2)

Today, let's consider some strangers we've come across in the past. Have you ever entertained angels? Did you ever wonder if the homeless person with whom you chatted was real or an angel in disguise? That possibility is encouragement enough to continue to show our hospitality. Joy in angels in disguise.

#MoreJesusMoreJoy365AngelinDisquise

April

11

"We do this by keeping our eyes on Jesus, the champion who initiates and perfects our faith. Because of the joy awaiting him, he endured the cross, disregarding its shame. Now he is seated in the place of honor beside God's throne." (Hebrews 12:2)

Today, let's look at the joy set before Jesus and how He endured the cross for our benefit. For His suffering, our joy was revealed. In what ways have you been obedient to God and joy was revealed? Joy in His obedience.

#MoreJesusMoreJoy365HisObedience

April

12

"How do you know what your life will be like tomorrow? Your life is like the morning fog— it's here a little while, then it's gone." (James 4:14)

Today, we are reminded that tomorrow may never come. Let's live today for Jesus and do the things we've always wanted to do. What are your God-given goals? Joy in living today for God.

#MoreJesusMoreJoy365LiveForHim

April

13

"Joyful are people of integrity, who follow the instructions of the LORD." (Psalm 119:1)

Today, let's nominate a person of integrity to commend for following Jesus. I think we've all seen someone whose cup is overflowing with joy, and you know it is because of the time that person spends with Jesus. That special someone is overflowing because she is praying to Him, listening to His instructions and living it out in her life. You know the person who is sure not to join in the laughter of a bad joke or gossip. Those kind of people stand out and are full of integrity for following Jesus' instructions. Who's your nominee? Joy in integrity.

#MoreJesusMoreJoy365integrity

April

14

"For we are God's masterpiece. He has created us anew in Christ Jesus, so we can do the good things he planned for us long ago." (Ephesians 2:10)

Today, let's just be reminded that we are a unique masterpiece created by God. Share a unique selfie, or a selfie that shows you are completing the things He planned long ago for your life. God sees in you a masterpiece. Joy in being a one of a kind.

#MoreJesusMoreJoy365HisMasterpiece

April

15

"If you forgive those who sin against you, your heavenly Father will forgive you." (Matthew 6:14)

Today, let's consider those against whom we may hold a grudge and ask Jesus for help to forgive them. Write yourself an apology note from your grudge. Read it aloud. Hear your words and imagine they came from the one against whom you have a grudge. Decide to forgive the one who sinned against you—just as Jesus forgave you. Share additional ways to forgive others. Joy in releasing grudges.

#MoreJesusMoreJoy365NoGrudges

April

16

"May all my thoughts be pleasing to him, for I rejoice in the LORD." (Psalm 104:34)

Today, choose a portion of scripture you want to know better. Write it out and read it throughout the day. Meditate on it all day and night. These thoughts are pleasing to the Lord. What scripture did you choose? Joy in thinking of the Lord.

#MoreJesusMoreJoy365MeditatingHisWord

April
17

*"'Yes, come,' Jesus said. So Peter went over the
side of the boat and walked on the water toward
Jesus."* (Matthew 14:29)

Today, let's go to God in prayer about this scripture. What is
God asking you to do? Is He asking you to step out in faith in
a certain area of your life? When we keep our eyes on Jesus,
we can do anything—just like Peter. Will you walk on the
water with Jesus? Joy in believing in Jesus.

#MoreJesusMoreJoy365WalkOnWater

April
18

*"David triumphed over Goliath with a sling and
a stone."* (1 Samuel 17:50, emphasis mine)

Today, pick up a stone and put it in your pocket. Whoever or
whatever your Goliath is today, find joy knowing your God
has already gone before you and gives you strength. Let the
stone in your pocket be a reminder that your Goliath has no
power! Show us your pocket stone. Joy in His strength.

#MoreJesusMoreJoy365HisStrength

April

19

"A gentle answer deflects anger, but harsh words make tempers flare." (Proverbs 15:1)

Today, let's listen and pause before talking or answering others. Practice gentleness in your replies to others and the peace of practicing the pause. How many times did you get to practice the pause? Joy in gentle words.

#MoreJesusMoreJoy365pause

April

20

"For Christ has already accomplished the purpose for which the law was given. As a result, all who believe in him are made right with God." (Romans 10:4)

Today, let's consider laws, both public and personal. Are you following God's laws? Which ones are easy and not so easy? Jesus is the ultimate Law Breaker. He defied death and is the law to follow. Joy in the Law.

#MoreJesusMoreJoy365TheLaw

April

21

"You show that you are a letter from Christ, the result of our ministry, written not with ink but with the Spirit of the living God, not on tablets of stone but on tablets of human hearts." (2 Corinthians 3:3, NIV)

Today, let's write a love letter to Jesus like He is the only One in the world who has our attention. Write to Him with your deepest gratitude for what He has done, does, and will do for you. Show us your stationery. Joy in writing love letters to God.

#MoreJesusMoreJoy365LoveLetters

April

22

"Think of it—the LORD is ready to heal me! I will sing his praises with instruments every day of my life in the Temple of the LORD." (Isaiah 38:20)

Today, let's examine this scripture and bring it full circle in the modern-day house of the Lord, the church. As we gather with other believers, let's lift up a song of praise. Share your pics of God's people singing in the house of the Lord. Joy in singing to the Lord all the days of your life.

#MoreJesusMoreJoy365ChurchSinging

April 23

"Then Jesus said to the woman, 'Your sins are forgiven.'" (Luke 7:48)

Today, let's see what sin and the forgiveness of sin really looks like. You will need vinegar (any kind), honey, and bread. Dip a piece of bread into the vinegar, and eat it to see what your sin tastes like. Then dip a piece of bread into honey and let your taste buds rejoice in what the forgiveness of sin tastes like. How did you feel about your sin and forgiven sins? Joy in being forgiven.

#MoreJesusMoreJoy365forgiven

April 24

"When he stops, the earth shakes. When he looks, the nations tremble. He shatters the everlasting mountains and levels the eternal hills. He is the Eternal One!" (Habakkuk 3:6)

Today, let's reflect on the awesome power of God. Nothing compares to His strength. Lift up a hand of praise to our Creator who strongly marches on before us. Describe His incredible power. Joy in a powerful God.

#MoreJesusMoreJoy365GodsPower

April

25

"God chose him as your ransom long before the world began, but now in these last days he has been revealed for your sake." (1 Peter 1:20)

Today, let's pause to look into a mirror, deep into your eyes and say, "Precious you—bought by His blood" As you pass a mirror throughout the day, pause for a second, look right into your eyes created by God and claim your truth. Show us your truth. Joy in His redemption.

#MoreJesusMoreJoy365redemption

April

26

"If you need wisdom, ask our generous God, and he will give it to you. He will not rebuke you for asking." (James 1:5)

Today, let's look up a question in the Bible you've always wondered about the answer. Use the index in the back to search by subject. Maybe it's tithing or fasting. Read and investigate until God shows you the answer. Share what you investigated. Joy in God-given answers.

#MoreJesusMoreJoy365GodAnswers

April

27

"But now you must be holy in everything you do, just as God who chose you is holy. For the Scriptures say, "You must be holy because I am holy." (1 Peter 1:15, 16)

Today, let's examine the definition of *holy*. The Bible tells us that God's children are dedicated to God for a purpose, that we are set aside, and different. Being holy is God's gift to us, just like grace. We are made holy in our acceptance and trust of Jesus. Are you holy? God gave us the Holy Spirit to help us overcome sin and live holy lives. Joy in being holy.

#MoreJesusMoreJoy365holy

April

28

"I have told you all this so that you may have peace in me. Here on earth you will have many trials and sorrows. But take heart, because I have overcome the world." (John 16:33)

Today, let's rejoice, knowing that we face nothing that Jesus hasn't already faced and *conquered*. Let's follow in His footsteps and know we're not alone. Where are His footsteps leading you? Joy in a mighty Conqueror.

#MoreJesusMoreJoy365conqueror

April
29

"And let us not neglect our meeting together, as some people do, but encourage one another, especially now that the day of his return is drawing near." (Hebrews 10:25)

Today, let's look at the importance of meeting together in church. Jesus asks us not to neglect meeting together because He wants us to encourage and strengthen one another in community. What do you look forward to at church? Is it the music, the message, or the holy hug the Holy Spirit gives you? Joy in community.

#MoreJesusMoreJoy365community

April
30

"For the whole law can be summed up in this one command: "Love your neighbor as yourself." (Galatians 5:14)

Today, let's look for the good in others. It's easy to see others' faults, but Jesus asks us to look for the good in others and to love them like we love and care for ourselves. Everyone is our *neighbor,* so we should extend our love to others everywhere we go—especially on social media. How can we show love to our neighbors? When we love others, we're made *right* with God. Joy in loving others.

#MoreJesusMoreJoy365neighbor

May

1

"Then God said, 'Let the land sprout with vegetation—every sort of seed-bearing plant, and trees that grow seed-bearing fruit. These seeds will then produce the kinds of plants and trees from which they came.' And that is what happened." (Genesis 1:11)

Today, let's imagine that God laughs in flowers. Just think about all the vegetation that He has created. Can you imagine His delicately and purposefully creating each individual species of flowers? Which of His creations of foliage bring you the most joy? Joy in His flowers.

#MoreJesusMoreJoy365GodLaughs

May

2

"'To whom will you compare me? Who is my equal?' asks the Holy One." (Isaiah 40:25)

Today, let's have an idol check. Have we placed anyone or anything into God's number-one slot? Sometimes life's struggles and challenges slip in our hearts and redirect our minds. Let's renew and declare today that Jesus Christ is Lord of all and Lord over us. There is no equal. Joy in Jesus as number one.

#MoreJesusMoreJoy365NoEqual

May

3

"Do you not know that in a race all the runners run, but only one gets the prize? Run in such a way as to get the prize." (1 Corinthians 9:24, NIV)

Today, let's write ourselves a love note from God. Write something like: "Dear One, I see you today and all your days. I am proud to be your Father. I know you face struggles, but through them, you choose Me. As your Papa, that's the best feeling. Keep going, dear one, run in such a way as to get the prize. Love, God." Joy in running the race all the way to Heaven.

#MoreJesusMoreJoy365RunTheRace

May

4

"Let everyone see that you are considerate in all you do. Remember, the Lord is coming soon." (Philippians 4:5)

Today, let's bask in our ultimate joy; the Lord is near. Invite Him intentionally everywhere you go. You will radiate joy with the Lord near you, and everyone will see Him through you. Where will you two go today? Joy in the nearness of God.

#MoreJesusMoreJoy365NearnessOfGod

May

5

"Without wise leadership, a nation falls; there is safety in having many advisers." (Proverbs 11:14)

Today, let's be mindful of leaders in our community. Think of someone who is leading by a great example and thank the person for his or her service. This individual could be a sports coach, a troop leader, a dance instructor, and so on. Send a text, an email, or a social media post. Who is a great leader among your community? Go out of your way to recognize wise leadership. Joy in wise counsel.

#MoreJesusMoreJoy365WiseCounsel

May

6

"We who are strong ought to bear with the failings of the weak and not to please ourselves." (Romans 15:1, NIV)

Today, let's write a nurse a note of encouragement. This nurse could be actively serving or one who has cared for you in the past—maybe even a friend or a family member. Nurses often help us when we cannot help ourselves. Who has helped you in your time of need? Joy in help when we are weak.

#MoreJesusMoreJoy365WhenWeak

May
7

"This is my command—be strong and courageous! Do not be afraid or discouraged. For the LORD your God is with you wherever you go." (Joshua 1:9)

Today, let's think about the missionaries that God has placed in some dangerous places. Maybe your church or a local business supports missionaries in the United States and around the world. Pray for them, reach out to them on social media, or send a letter to encourage them. Tell them you're praying for their safety and for God to strengthen them in any situation. Who are your missionaries, and where are they serving? Joy in missionaries.

#MoreJesusMoreJoy365missions

May
8

"If you look for me wholeheartedly, you will find me." (Jeremiah 29:13)

Today, let's praise God for open communication. Jesus is always there for us and hears every one of our prayers. We can seek Him any time of the day, and He is waiting for us. We will find Him when we wholeheartedly seek Him. When, where, and how do you seek Him? Joy in seeking the Lord.

#MoreJesusMoreJoy365SeekHim

May

9

"For I am not ashamed of this Good News about Christ. It is the power of God at work, saving everyone who believes." (Romans 1:16)

Today, let's raise it up and lift it high and let your Jesus-freak flag fly. Proclaim that we are not ashamed of the gospel of Jesus Christ! Share this truth about your faith in a social media post or in a conversation as the Holy Spirit permits. How will you declare your truth? Joy in proclaiming your salvation.

#MoreJesusMoreJoy365IamNotAshamed

May

10

"Then you will experience God's peace, which exceeds anything we can understand. His peace will guard your hearts and minds as you live in Christ Jesus." (Philippians 4:7)

Today, let's go after that peace that Jesus so freely gives us. We can achieve His peace when we realize that God is in control, and we are not. Tell Him this simple truth in prayer. Praying to Him includes Him in our lives, and we are never lonely. Prayer allows Him to guide our lives. Let's share this truth: God is in control. Joy in His peace.

#MoreJesusMoreJoy365HisPeace

May

11

"They weep as they go to plant their seed, but they sing as they return with the harvest." (Psalm 126:6)

Today, let's plant some seeds and watch them grow. Maybe it's a patio tomato plant, a windowsill herb box, or a new plant from the grocery store. Let your choice be a reminder to cultivate our relationship with Jesus because He is the only One who can turn our tears into life-giving joy. Show us your seeds of joy. Water and watch it grow. Joy in growth.

#MoreJesusMoreJoy365growth

May

12

"We were filled with laughter, and we sang for joy. And the other nations said, 'What amazing things the LORD has done for them.'" (Psalm 126:2)

Today, let's do some car singing and dancing. Kick out your best moves, the sprinkler, and the robot at the next red traffic light. Show the nations of people what joy looks like. What are your best moves and songs? Make someone's day by bringing a smile and laughter. Joy is knowing Jesus.

#MoreJesusMoreJoy365CarDancing

May

13

"Your love has given me much joy and comfort, my brother, for your kindness has often refreshed the hearts of God's people." (Philemon 1:7)

Today, let's be a refresher of souls, a spring of never-ending living water that encourages everyone we meet, including co-workers, strangers, friends, kids, and spouses. Look for ways to refresh others through a kind word, a compliment, encouragement or just a flashy smile; they all go a long way. What are some of your refreshing ways to show kindness? Joy in kindness.

#MoreJesusMoreJoy365kindness

May

14

"In the beginning the Word already existed. The Word was with God, and the Word was God." (John 1:1, 2)

Today, let's celebrate the Word of God. Jesus, fully man and fully God, always existed as the Word. Jesus was the walking Word sent by God to teach us. Do you have the Word of God in your house, your hand, and your heart? Joy in the Word of God.

#MoreJesusMoreJoy365WordOfGod

May

15

"No discipline seems pleasant at the time, but painful. Later on, however, it produces a harvest of righteousness and peace for those who have been trained by it." (Hebrews 12:11)

Today, let's remember that God loves us enough to show us the error of our ways. He does this so we can be kinder to one another in love. Even though His lessons are not always pleasant, we are joyful with a changed heart from it. In what areas of your life are you being, or have you been, disciplined by God? Joy in God's discipline.

#MoreJesusMoreJoy365discipline

May

16

"For his anger lasts only a moment, but his favor lasts a lifetime! Weeping may last through the night, but joy comes with the morning." (Psalm 30:5)

Today, let's think back to a time when God was angry with you, and you knew it. Not a good feeling, but thankfully, it doesn't last long. He quickly disciplined, and we stepped back in line. It is the teaching spirit of God. How did you feel when God's anger disappeared? Joy in the morning.

#MoreJesusMoreJoy365MorningJoy

May

17

"If you have encouragement from being united with Christ, if any comfort from his love, sharing in the Spirit, with tenderness and compassion, then make my joy complete by being like-minded, having the same love, being one in spirit and of one mind." (Philippians 2:1, 2, NIV)

Today, let's search our minds to see where we need His joy in our life. Is it your finances, your friendships? In prayer, ask God for His joy to reign in you, over you and through you. Take steps to cultivate that joy and to be united with others. Joy in being likeminded in Jesus.

#MoreJesusMoreJoy365LikeMinded

May

18

"He counts the stars and calls them all by name." (Psalm 147:4)

Today, let's plan to go outside and stargaze. How many stars can you count? It is so hard to imagine that God counts the stars and knows them all by name. How much better do you think He knows us whom He created in His image? Joy under the stars.

#MoreJesusMoreJoy365StarGazing

May

19

"Dear brothers and sisters, when troubles of any kind come your way, consider it an opportunity for great joy. For you know that when your faith is tested, your endurance has a chance to grow." (James 1:2, 3)

Today, let's share how our faith has been tested and endured during trials. Remember, you can share with a picture, one word, or whatever brings joy to your heart. In our trials Jesus has the opportunity to grow and shape us. Consider it great joy because of your faith in Jesus who will always be with you and help you get through it. Joy in faith unthinkable.

#MoreJesusMoreJoy365faith

May

20

"Create in me a clean heart, O God. Renew a loyal spirit within me." (Psalm 51:10)

Today, let's raise our white flags and ask for a clean heart to be created in us. When we surrender all that we are to Jesus, He will create a clean heart in us. Will you raise your white flag high? Joy in a clean heart from God.

#MoreJesusMoreJoy365cleanheart

May 21

"But the Holy Spirit produces this kind of fruit in our lives: love, joy, peace, patience, kindness, goodness, faithfulness." (Galatians 5:22)

Today, let's look at how we can attain all the fruits that the Holy Spirit gives. When we spend time with Jesus getting to know Him through praying, reading His Word, and loving Him, we obtain the fruit of the Spirit. Which of these fruit are produced in your life and which ones would you like the Holy Spirit to give you? Joy in the fruit of the Holy Spirit.

#MoreJesusMoreJoy365FruitOfTheSpirit

May 22

"That is why we never give up. Though our bodies are dying, our spirits are being renewed every day." (2 Corinthians 4:16)

Today, let's face it. Who doesn't want to be renewed and made new again, have a fresh beginning, or a do-over every day? Spending time daily with Jesus does exactly that; it renews. Schedule your daily meeting with Him; you won't want to miss it! When do you meet with Him? Joy in His renewals.

#MoreJesusMoreJoy365renew

May 23

"The LORD will guide you always; he will satisfy your needs in a sun-scorched land and will strengthen your frame. You will be like a well-watered garden, like a spring whose waters never fail." (Isaiah 58:11, NIV)

Today, let's take a look at ourselves and take the guidance that the Lord is giving to us. He instructs us during our time spent with Him. Are we a well-watered garden or a sun-scorched land? His replenishing waters will never run dry. Joy in His guidance.

#MoreJesusMoreJoy365HisGuidance

May 24

"Work hard so you can present yourself to God and receive his approval. Be a good worker, one who does not need to be ashamed and who correctly explains the word of truth." (2 Timothy 2:15)

Today, let's look at how to study God's Word. To explain the Word of God, you must spend time studying it. What is the best Bible study you've ever done? Why was it so special to you? What did you learn the most? Joy studying the Word of God.

#MoreJesusMoreJoy365Study

May

25

"But now, O Jacob, listen to the LORD who created you. O Israel, the one who formed you says, 'Do not be afraid, for I have ransomed you. I have called you by name; you are mine.'"
(Isaiah 43:1)

Today, let's find joy in simply knowing Jesus knows our name, and we are important to Him. Share your name and how you got it. Maybe yours is a nickname or a namesake. Maybe your gender surprised your parents, and they had to scramble at the last minute to name you. Joy in being known by Him.

#MoreJesusMoreJoy365HeKnowsMyName

May

26

"The LORD himself will fight for you. Just stay calm."
(Exodus 14:14)

Today, let's celebrate just knowing the Lord will always show up and fight our battles. We need only to trust Him and be calm to let Him work. When we don't see a way out and are full of despair, we can turn to God and ask for His help, protection, and love. How has the Lord fought your battles? Joy in being calm.

#MoreJesusMoreJoy365HeFightsForMe

May 27

"One of them, when he saw that he was healed, came back to Jesus, shouting, 'Praise God!' He fell to the ground at Jesus' feet, thanking him for what he had done. This man was a Samaritan. Jesus asked, 'Didn't I heal ten men? Where are the other nine? Has no one returned to give glory to God except this foreigner?'" (Luke 17:15-18)

Today, let's use these two words more often: *thank you*. It seems so easy to say, but so often we fail to say *thank you* to God and to others. Practice looking at the eyes of the cashier or wait staff and politely say, "Thank you." Whether in prayer or in person, how many times can you find to say "Thank you" for something today? Joy in saying *thank you*.

#MoreJesusMoreJoy365ThankYou

May 28

"There is no greater love than to lay down one's life for one's friends." (John 15:13)

Today, let's go out of our way and thank those who are in active military service, veterans, and their family. Thank them on social media, write a note, or phone. Let them know that when one serves, all serve, and you're thankful for their service. Joy in selfless service.

#MoreJesusMoreJoy365SelflessService

May 29

"Then God said, 'I am giving you a sign of my covenant with you and with all living creatures, for all generations to come. I have placed my rainbow in the clouds. It is the sign of my covenant with you and with all the earth.'"
(Genesis 9:12, 13)

Today, let's be reminded the next time we see a rainbow that it's God's promise that He will never again flood the entire earth. Every time it rains, God flashes up a rainbow to remind us He will not flood us. What a beautiful promise to see. How many times have you seen God's promise flying the skies? Show us your favorite rainbow. Joy in the covenant of the rainbow.

#MoreJesusMoreJoy365RainbowRule

May 30

"For you are all children of God through faith in Christ Jesus." (Galatians 3:26)

Today, let's celebrate that we believers are children of God. We have been adopted by royalty. Are you living as royalty or as an orphan? Through our faith in Jesus, we are orphans no more. Joy in being adopted by royalty.

#MoreJesusMoreJoy365AdoptedByRoyalty

May

31

"All Scripture is God-breathed and is useful for teaching, rebuking, correcting and training in righteousness." (2 Timothy 3:16, NIV)

Today, let's look at scripture. All scripture was written with divine inspiration from God. It is alive, God-breathed. Joy fills the air in heaven. When we are connected to God, we are connected to His Joy. Through the Bible, God communicates with us through both teaching and correcting. How have you experienced joy through His teaching? Joy in scripture.

#MoreJesusMoreJoy365scripture

June

1

"When Moses came down Mount Sinai carrying the two stone tablets inscribed with the terms of the covenant, he wasn't aware that his face had become radiant because he had spoken to the Lord." (Exodus 34:29)

Today, let's spend some time with God and have it be a one-way type of day. You read and listen as He talks. Then you will radiate like Moses from your time spent with Him. Show us your God-glow selfie. Joy in God's glow.

#MoreJesusMoreJoy365radiate

June

2

"And if foreigners living among you want to celebrate the Passover to the LORD, they must follow these same decrees and regulations. The same laws apply both to native-born Israelites and to the foreigners living among you." (Numbers 9:14)

Today, let's think back to the last house guest or dinner guest you had. Did you skip blessing the food or going to church because you didn't want to offend or make your guest feel uncomfortable? That stuff is easy to do, but God is asking us to live out our convictions regardless of who is around us. Don't change how you pray and when you worship God. Model His behavior to others; let them see Him through you. Joy in honoring Him always.

#MoreJesusMoreJoy365HonorAlways

June

3

"Remember to observe the Sabbath day by keeping it holy." (Exodus 20:8)

Today, let's be reminded that the Sabbath equals rest from work. God gave us Sundays to rest, refresh, and remember Him. How do you do Sundays with the Lord? Joy in rest.

#MoreJesusMoreJoy365rest

June 4

"When all the Israelites saw the Ark of the Covenant of the LORD coming into the camp, their shout of joy was so loud it made the ground shake!" (1 Samuel 4:5)

Today, let's shout for joy like those in the Old Testament. The Israelites were so excited to have the ark of the covenant back, they rejoiced so loudly that the ground shook. Have you ever been so joyful that you made the ground shake—or so it seemed? Maybe it was a surprise party or a joyous reunion. Joy in shouting it.

#MoreJesusMoreJoy365ShoutJoy

June 5

"And this is love: that we walk in obedience to his commands. As you have heard from the beginning, his command is that you walk in love." (2 John 6, NIV)

Today, we are reminded yet again how to love. Jesus asked us to practice loving others. We love when we don't judge others, do serve others, and accept people for who they are right where they're at. How do you walk in love? Joy in practicing love.

#MoreJesusMoreJoy365PracticeLove

June
6

"For God has not given us a spirit of fear and timidity, but of power, love, and self-discipline." (2 Timothy 1:7)

Today, let's claim the power that God so freely gives us through the Holy Spirit. We have power, love, and self-discipline to keep going in our faith journey. Jesus calls us to be bold. Are you a sidewalk prophet or do you gently correct someone's misconception about God? What does your boldness looks like? Joy in the boldness of faith.

#MoreJesusMoreJoy365bold

June
7

"You will show me the way of life, granting me the joy of your presence and the pleasures of living with you forever." (Psalm 16:11)

Today, let's express our joy that we have eternal life! This world cannot offer us the eternal life that Jesus can. Enter Jesus' presence and share your life with Him. Share your joy of living now in the presence of God forever. Joy in His presence.

#MoreJesusMoreJoy365HisPresence

June

8

"Let us think of ways to motivate one another to acts of love and good works." (Hebrews 10:24)

Today, let's consider someone we know who needs lifting up. Let's prayerfully consider how you may encourage the person to keep going. Did God give you scripture to send or an errand to run for this person? Life is a team sport; don't leave anybody behind. Joy in lifting others.

#MoreJesusMoreJoy365LiftingOthers

June

9

"They were calling out to each other, 'Holy, holy, holy is the LORD of Heaven's Armies! The whole earth is filled with his glory!'" (Isaiah 6:3)

Today, let's be full of His glory and declare it! The Bible describes glory as to honor in praise and worship, God who is full of splendor and majestic beauty. How will you worship Jesus today? Joy in His glory.

#MoreJesusMoreJoy365HisGlory

June 10

"Even though the fig trees have no blossoms, and there are no grapes on the vines; even though the olive crop fails, and the fields lie empty and barren; even though the flocks die in the fields, and the cattle barns are empty, yet I will rejoice in the LORD! I will be joyful in the God of my salvation!" (Habakkuk 3:17, 18)

Today, while proclaiming joy's truth, let's state what we are missing in our life. Even though we are out of some of the things we want or need right now, see through it to the truth of what Jesus has already done for us. Choose to celebrate in your heart what He will do tomorrow. Joy in faith in God.

#MoreJesusMoreJoy365FaithInGod

June 11

"Light is sweet; how pleasant to see a new day dawning." (Ecclesiastes 11:7)

Today, let's take a five-minute break and sit in the sun. Cloudy or rainy, grab an umbrella and relax anyway. Sit in God's presence, and let His light warm your bones. Show us your new day dawning. Joy in the light of day.

#MoreJesusMoreJoy365LightOfDay

June

12

"Who else has held the oceans in his hand? Who has measured off the heavens with his fingers? Who else knows the weight of the earth or has weighed the mountains and hills on a scale?" (Isaiah 40:12)

Today, let's imagine what it took for God to create our habitat…and us. What is your favorite part of His creation? Is it marveling at His majestic mountains, gazing at the rolling oceans, or standing in awe of the life He created who is dear to you? Joy in the creation of the world.

#MoreJesusMoreJoy365HisCreations

June

13

"The generous will prosper; those who refresh others will themselves be refreshed." (Proverbs 11:25)

Today, let's be reminded that everything we have belongs to God. Since everything is His, let's use His gifts to refresh others. How can you be a helping hand on this day? Maybe it's buying someone's coffee, putting money in a washer at the Laundromat, or paying for the groceries belonging to the person behind you. As we share with others, the Lord replenishes those gifts. Joy in refreshing others.

#MoreJesusMoreJoy365RefreshOthers

June

14

"Fix these words of mine in your hearts and minds. Write them on the doorframes of your houses and on your gates." (Deuteronomy 11:18, 20)

Today, let's see who has already done this. Do you have something like this already on your front doors, gates, or entryway? If not, what would you like yours to say about the Lord? When we fortify our lives with scripture, then all will see and know that the Lord dwells here. Joy in fortified scripture.

#MoreJesusMoreJoy365FortifiedScripture

June

15

"You must have the same attitude that Christ Jesus had." (Philippians 2:5)

Today, let's look at the character of Jesus. We know He was a humble servant who loved everyone. Do you have a servant's attitude? Do you walk humbly with others as you serve them? Which is your favorite lesson from our humble servant Jesus? Joy in the attributes of Jesus.

#MoreJesusMoreJoy365HumbleServant

June 16

"Don't be like them, for your Father knows exactly what you need even before you ask him!" (Matthew 6:8)

Today, let's look at the character of God and His massive knowledge. He already knows what we need before we even ask Him. Even though He knows our needs, He still wants to hear from us. Sometimes just a quiet look toward Heaven with a hand held high is all the expression God needs to know what's going on in our hearts. How do you pray to God? Joy in His knowledge.

#MoreJesusMoreJoy365FatherKnows

June 17

"The LORD is good to those who depend on him, to those who search for him." (Lamentations 3:25)

Today, let's smile, knowing we have a good Father. We who search for Him are dependent on Him and wait for His guidance. For what reason will you seek Jesus? What will your prayers or praises be? Joy in a good Father.

#MoreJesusMoreJoy365GoodFather

June

18

"So I decided there is nothing better than to enjoy food and drink and to find satisfaction in work. Then I realized that these pleasures are from the hand of God. For who can eat or enjoy anything apart from him?" (Ecclesiastes 2:24, 25)

Today, let's invite someone to a picnic breakfast, lunch or dinner. It doesn't have to be fancy; it can be Pop Tarts and soda if you want. Whatever you put in a picnic basket is already fun and tasty. Give thanks to God and bless the food. Show us your picnic. Joy in sharing a meal together.

#MoreJesusMoreJoy365ShareAMeal

June

19

"Then God said, 'Let the waters beneath the sky flow together into one place, so dry ground may appear.' And that is what happened." (Genesis 1:9)

Today, let's be mindful of each step you take. As you look down, also look out at the land which God has created for you to roam about. Show us your favorite dry stomping grounds. Joy in His land.

#MoreJesusMoreJoy365DryGround

June

20

"Salt is good for seasoning. But if it loses its flavor, how do you make it salty again? You must have the qualities of salt among yourselves and live in peace with each other." (Mark 9:50)

Today, let's add salt to whatever we're eating—just for today. Be reminded that we are a salty flavoring used by God to flavor the earth. As salt changes the flavor of food, we too can be the change that's needed in our world. Let's stay salty, and remember we are set apart and are a different flavor of the earth. Be salty. Show us your salt. Joy in being different than the world.

#MoreJesusMoreJoy365BeSalty

June

21

"Look to the LORD and his strength; seek his face always." (1 Chronicles 16:11, NIV)

Today, let's spend some time daydreaming about what the face of God looks like. I bet your face will glow just thinking these joyous thoughts about God. Oh, the awe and wonder of the One and only God! Describe His face. Joy in dreaming of Him.

#MoreJesusMoreJoy365DreamingOfJesus

June

22

"I was there when he set the limits of the seas, so they would not spread beyond their boundaries. And when he marked off the earth's foundations." (Proverbs 8:29)

Today, let's gaze into the waters with gratitude. Each time you wash your hands, do dishes, or prepare your food, thank God for the mighty, flowing waters. God told the water that it could only go this far and no farther. Have you experienced the boundaries of water at the ocean, lake, or pond? Joy in creation's boundaries.

#MoreJesusMoreJoy365boundaries

June

23

"But those who drink the water I give will never be thirsty again. It becomes a fresh, bubbling spring within them, giving them eternal life." (John 4:14)

Today, let's reflect back to the day you drank from the *spring of living water*. How were your eyes opened when you first believed in Jesus? Who was with you on your first day journey? If today is the day, then welcome home! Joy in a quenched soul.

#MoreJesusMoreJoy365ThirstNoMore

June 24

"But Jesus often withdrew to lonely places and prayed." (Luke 5:16, NIV)

Today, let's sneak off to a private place and pray to Jesus—like He prayed to His Father. Maybe it's a park bench, a patch of green grass, or leaning against a special tree. Maybe you have a prayer room or a secret garden. Find your place and find Jesus. Show us your place. Joy in the solitude of prayer.

#MoreJesusMoreJoy365Lonelyplaces

June 25

"A cheerful heart is good medicine, but a broken spirit saps a person's strength." (Proverbs 17:22)

Today, let's bum a piece of gum or get some good chewing gum. Get the kind that blows the biggest bubbles that smack and pop, and catch in your hair – that kind. Take a bubble-gum selfie, and share the joy. Joy in a cheerful heart.

#MoreJesusMoreJoy365CheerfulHeart

June

26

"But Jesus said, 'Let the children come to me. Don't stop them! For the Kingdom of Heaven belongs to those who are like these children.'" (Matthew 19:14)

Today, let's go outside and blow some bubbles to connect with our inner child. We know children are dependent on their earthly father. Let's remember that God's children will never be so grown up that they aren't dependent on Him. How did you connect with your inner child today? Joy in dependence of Jesus.

#MoreJesusMoreJoy365dependence

June

27

"We love because he first loved us." (1 John 4:19, NIV)

Today, let's pick a flower from the ground or the grocery store. Gaze into the petals as you pluck each one, saying *"He Loves Me," "He Loves Me, etc"* No need today for a "He loves me not" because He is so full of never-ending love for us. What a fun exercise to do with kids and youth! Joy in being His first love.

#MoreJesusMoreJoy365FirstLove

June

28

"When I look at the night sky and see the work of your fingers—the moon and the stars you set in place—what are mere mortals that you should think about them, human beings that you should care for them?" (Psalm 8:3, 4)

Tonight, let's go on a mission to lie in the green grass and stargaze. Allow yourself to imagine how God created the entire earth. Pause on day 4 when God created the sun, the moon and the stars to shine down, and consider His majesty. Joy in the greatness of God.

#MoreJesusMoreJoy365GodsGreatness

June

29

"Teach me your ways, O LORD, that I may live according to your truth! Grant me purity of heart, so that I may honor you." (Psalm 86:11)

Today, let's memorize this scripture. Write it out, decorate it, and place it somewhere prominent and easily seen. A pure heart is a heart faithful in always following God. Joy in purity of heart.

#MoreJesusMoreJoy365PurityOfHeart

June

30

"Remember, it is sin to know what you ought to do and then not do it." (James 4:17)

Today, let's not turn our heads away from the difficulties of life. Let's look up and reach out to do the good from which we often sulk away. Maybe that's helping out a friend in need, stopping for a chat with the homeless or walking the dogs at the shelter. What is God putting on your heart and in your path today? Joy in responsible goodness.

#MoreJesusMoreJoy365goodness

July

1

"A person finds joy in giving an apt reply—and how good is a timely word!" (Proverbs 15:23, NIV)

Today, let's be the first one to give apt reply. Set the tone and opening for joy to reign in conversations with others. Which words did you use? Build up one another for the kingdom of God. Joy in a timely word.

#MoreJesusMoreJoy365TimelyWords

July

2

"But it is no shame to suffer for being a Christian. Praise God for the privilege of being called by his name!" (1 Peter 4:16)

Today, let's take pride in His name, smile big, and proclaim it! Share His name today in conversation when the Holy Spirit permits or in social media or in any way your heart desires. Joy in bearing His name.

#MoreJesusMoreJoy365JesusName

July

3

"For you have been called to live in freedom, my brothers and sisters. But don't use your freedom to satisfy your sinful nature. Instead, use your freedom to serve one another in love." (Galatians 5:13)

Today, let's proclaim our freedom. To be truly free is to have freedom from sin, and only Jesus can give us this gift. Being freed from our sinful ways is amazing, which, in turn, gives us freedom to serve someone other than our self, i.e., serve others. How long have you been free? Serving others is serving God Himself. Joy in freedom.

#MoreJesusMoreJoy365freedom

July

4

"What joy for the nation whose God is the LORD, whose people he has chosen as his inheritance." (Psalm 33:12)

Today, let's fly our nation's flag and declare that Jesus is Lord of all. Joyful are the people who accepted God for they trust, love, and obey Him. We claimed Him, and He called us His. Joy in His heritage.

#MoreJesusMoreJoy365HisHeritage

July

5

"for through him God created everything in the heavenly realms and on earth. He made the things we can see and the things we can't see— such as thrones, kingdoms, rulers, and authorities in the unseen world. Everything was created through him and for him." (Colossians 1:16)

Today, let's look at the authority of Jesus who is holy and ruler over all. Jesus is the ruler of the visible physical world and also the invisible spiritual world. Is there an area you can see Him ruling? Is He the ruler over you? Joy in His authority.

#MoreJesusMoreJoy365AllAuthority

July

6

"When God's people are in need, be ready to help them. Always be eager to practice hospitality." (Romans 12:13)

Today, let's scan our life to see where God wants us to act and practice hospitality. Christian hospitality is all about making the guest feel welcomed or included. Let them know they have been heard and are important. Hospitality at its finest is loving others like Jesus loves us, which also makes us feel special. Share how God wants you to practice hospitality? Does it come easy for you or is it one of your gifts? Joy in hospitality.

#MoreJesusMoreJoy365hospitality

July

7

"And let the peace that comes from Christ rule in your hearts. For as members of one body you are called to live in peace. And always be thankful." (Colossians 3:15)

Today, let's be reminded to stay close to Jesus and to keep our peace. When tough life circumstances happen, we often give away our peace to worry and fear. But remember, we don't have to! We simply need to spend time with Jesus, telling Him our worries and fears, and allowing Him to rule in our hearts. Let's declare that *"He rules our hearts."* Joy living in peace.

#MoreJesusMoreJoy365AtPeace

July 8

"Come close to God, and God will come close to you. Wash your hands, you sinners; purify your hearts, for your loyalty is divided between God and the world." (James 4:8)

Today, let's forfeit the world and spend some quiet time listening for God's guidance. After you've asked Him for whatever need you have in prayer, practice listening to Him. Just be silent, knowing He is with you. How long did you forfeit the world today? Joy in the closeness of God.

#MoreJesusMoreJoy365ClosenessOfGod

July 9

"Then Christ will make his home in your hearts as you trust in him. Your roots will grow down into God's love and keep you strong." (Ephesians 3:17)

Today, let's rummage through the Christmas decorations and find one that is special to you. Place it where you will see it— maybe near the sink in the kitchen or in your bathroom. You can gaze at it whenever you see it, remembering His love has no limits. Show us your special decoration. Joy in Christmas every day.

#MoreJesusMoreJoy365ChristmasEveryDay

July 10

"From the rising of the sun to the place where it sets, the name of the LORD is to be praised." (Psalm 113:3, NIV)

Today, let's watch the sunset. It happens really fast, so check your sunset times and you don't miss it. Try to make yourself available to see it. If at work, take a quick three-minute break to take it in. If at home, those dishes will wait. Let God turn off the lights and tuck you in tonight. Show us your sunsets. Joy in praising Him as the sun sets.

#MoreJesusMoreJoy365sunsets

July 11

"Shout to the LORD, all the earth; break out in praise and sing for joy!" (Psalm 98:4)

Today, let's tune in to our favorite Christian radio station. KLOVE.com is a station broadcasted around the world. Let's sing along, knowing other Jesus followers are singing praises to Him too. Let your heart join with others and sing to God. What songs did you sing to Him? Joy in singing praises to God.

#MoreJesusMoreJoy365SingPraise

July

12

"Therefore, let us offer through Jesus a continual sacrifice of praise to God, proclaiming our allegiance to his name." (Hebrews 13:15)

Today, let's praise His holy name and offer our praise in the morning before our day gets too busy. Praise Him again at lunch when you have a few seconds to yourself, and at night you can praise Him for giving you another day. Cultivate joy in confession and praise. Share one of your prayers with us. Joy in proclaiming Jesus' name.

#MoreJesusMoreJoy365ProclaimingHisName

July

13

"Then Jesus took the loaves, gave thanks to God, and distributed them to the people. Afterward he did the same with the fish. And they all ate as much as they wanted." (John 6:11)

Today, let's ponder in awe over Jesus, who fed 5000 people with five loaves and two fish. In what ways has Jesus multiplied and provided for you, like He did with the loaves and fish? Joy in His provisions.

#MoreJesusMoreJoy365LoavesAndFish

July

14

"The LORD God placed the man in the Garden of Eden to tend and watch over it." (Genesis 2:15)

Today, let's be reminded that God created Adam to be our very first farmer. Let's recognize how hard farmers work and how great it is to have fresh food on our tables because of their labor! Thank a local farmer by purchasing locally grown food or drop them a note of gratitude for all of their hard work. Joy in working God's land.

#MoreJesusMoreJoy365farmer

July

15

"The name of the LORD is a strong fortress; the godly run to him and are safe." (Proverbs 18:10)

Today, let's just take a minute and admire the Lord's strength. He is the God who can move mountains and calm the seas with a mere motion of a finger. Let's remember His strength and run to Him whenever we need His help. When did you last run into the arms of Jesus? Joy in His arms.

#MoreJesusMoreJoy365HisArms

July

16

"I am the one who made the earth and created people to live on it. With my hands I stretched out the heavens. All the stars are at my command." (Isaiah 45:12)

Today, what is the one thing in God's creation that brings you the most joy? Is it your spouse, a friendship, a furry companion, or the flowers that God sends you every summer day? Joy in His creation.

#MoreJesusMoreJoy365FavoriteCreation

July

17

"We have this hope as an anchor for the soul, firm and secure." (Hebrews 6:19, NIV)

Today, let's put our hope in Jesus who anchors our souls and fills it with joy. An anchor steadies us when the waves crash on us. Just as the boat is anchored to stay in place, we too can anchor ourselves to Jesus and stay close to Him. Is your hope and anchor in Him? Show us your anchors. Joy in hope.

#MoreJesusMoreJoy365HopeAnchors

July

18

"In this new life, it doesn't matter if you are a Jew or a Gentile, circumcised or uncircumcised, barbaric, uncivilized, slave, or free. Christ is all that matters, and he lives in all of us." (Colossians 3:11)

Today, let's share that we are all united in Christ Jesus. There is no division of people under Jesus. There is no rank for race, income, or education level. For Christ is all and in all. Jesus accepts all who come to Him. What does His union look like to you? Joy in His union.

#MoreJesusMoreJoy365HisUnion

July

19

"You haven't done this before. Ask, using my name, and you will receive, and you will have abundant joy." (John 16:24)

Today, let's share some answered prayers. What have you requested from Him, and how has He answered you? Take delight in having a personal relationship with Jesus. Joy in answered prayers.

#MoreJesusMoreJoy365AnsweredPrayers

July 20

"So you, too, must show love to foreigners, for you yourselves were once foreigners in the land of Egypt." (Deuteronomy 10:19)

Today, let's remember that God calls us to love, simply love. To love, we must have a right heart with God. When we come to Him and confess our sins and ask for a changed heart, He forgives us and gives us one. With our new changed heart, we can use it to love everyone, especially foreigners, as He has asked us to do. *Everyone* has no limits, and no one is excluded. How do you show God's love to foreigners and welcome them? Joy in foreign love.

#MoreJesusMoreJoy365ForeignLove

July 21

"How great you are, O Sovereign LORD! There is no one like you. We have never even heard of another God like you!" (2 Samuel 7:22)

Today, let's consider David's prayer praise. Praising God in prayer is easy when we are passionate about a certain matter. When was the last time you prayed like that to God? For what were you praising Him? Joy in prayer praise.

#MoreJesusMoreJoy365PrayerPraise

July

22

"But when you ask him, be sure that your faith is in God alone. Do not waver, for a person with divided loyalty is as unsettled as a wave of the sea that is blown and tossed by the wind. Such people should not expect to receive anything from the Lord." (James 1:6, 7)

Today, let's become prayer warriors! As prayer warriors, we can boldly and confidently go before God with any request because of our faith in Him. When we warriors take to prayer, it is a full-on battle of the heart displayed before God. We petition Him with whatever we've got left and pray down our family by name, asking God to intervene. Are you a prayer warrior or do you want to become one? It is an honor and a privilege to pray for others, a comfort for us here on earth. Joy in being a confident prayer warrior.

#MoreJesusMoreJoy365PrayerWarrior

July

23

"So if the Son sets you free, you are truly free." (John 8:36)

Today, let's visualize Jesus as the chain breaker. He has the power to set us free from whatever sin entraps us. What chain did He break free for you? Confess your sins to Him today and let Him set you free. Joy in broken chains.

#MoreJesusMoreJoy365ChainBreaker

July

24

"But mightier than the violent raging of the seas, mightier than the breakers on the shore— the LORD above is mightier than these!" (Psalm 93:4)

Today, let's visualize the mighty waters of the ocean. If you've ever gazed at the ocean long enough, you're sure to realize that it is one powerful force, one that doesn't listen to anyone, and goes where it wants. Nothing can stop it. The Lord's power is mightier than these. What does the power of the Lord look like to you? Joy in a mighty God.

#MoreJesusMoreJoy365MightyGod

July

25

"For the Lord is the Spirit, and wherever the Spirit of the Lord is, there is freedom." (2 Corinthians 3:17)

Today, let's proclaim that we live free in Christ! Since Jesus came and made us free from sin's hold on us, we are free to live for Him, love like Him and be free with Him. Show us how you live free in Christ. Joy in His freedom.

#MoreJesusMoreJoy365LiveFreeInChrist

July 26

"So let's not get tired of doing what is good. At just the right time we will reap a harvest of blessing if we don't give up." (Galatians 6:9)

Today, let's share ways that we can keep going and never give up. It's hard to keep going when our work goes unnoticed, we don't receive praise, and we seldom hear "Thank you." But God sees everything; nothing we do goes unnoticed by Him. If we don't get a "Thank you" here, we will be sure to get one in Heaven where we will reap a harvest of righteousness. Keep going! Joy in never giving up.

#MoreJesusMoreJoy365NeverGiveUp

July 27

"But those who trust in the LORD will find new strength. They will soar high on wings like eagles. They will run and not grow weary. They will walk and not faint." (Isaiah 40:31)

Today, let's look at how we trust the Lord. When we trust the Lord, He gives us great strength to accomplish the things that we wouldn't normally be able to do—like working hard on missions trips without getting tired. He's working through us, and we trust Him to keep going. How has Jesus strengthened you when you most needed His strength? Joy in new strength.

#MoreJesusMoreJoy365NewStrength

July

28

"So God created human beings in his own image. In the image of God he created them; male and female he created them." (Genesis 1:27)

Today, let's consider all the colors of people that God has created and loves. Let's put on an outfit that contains all of the colors that God has created—or close to it. Wear them proudly and be reminded to love and respect every color of person because when we do, we are loving God's creation. God loves like nobody else, so let's live and love like nobody else. Joy in His one-of-a-kind love.

#MoreJesusMoreJoy365OneOfAKindLove

July

29

"Joyful is the person who finds wisdom, the one who gains understanding." (Proverbs 3:13)

Today, let's be reminded that we find knowledge when we read the Bible and gaining a new understanding brings us joy. Let's read the Bible out loud. Let your voice and ears catch up with your eyes. Read to yourself or find someone to read to. Joy in understanding God's Word.

#MoreJesusMoreJoy365understanding

July

30

"Charm is deceptive, and beauty does not last; but a woman who fears the LORD will be greatly praised." (Proverbs 31:30)

Today, let's look at what makes one lovely. We can talk to God daily and that alone will make us lovely and admirable. To fear the Lord in all ways is to be praised. Those of us who believe in God and obey Him will look differently than the world because we love and fear Him. Joy in fearing God.

#MoreJesusMoreJoy365FearGod

July

31

"Kind words are like honey—sweet to the soul and healthy for the body." (Proverbs 16:24)

Today, let's practice this truth and use as many kind words as we can today. Often, we use kind words in the form of compliments, but some additional *kind* words include, "Please," "Thank you," and "Tell me more." How many kind words did you offer? Joy in kind words.

#MoreJesusMoreJoy365KindWords

August 1

"Those who live at the ends of the earth stand in awe of your wonders. From where the sun rises to where it sets, you inspire shouts of joy." (Psalm 65:8)

Today, let's scour the Bible for scriptures containing the word *joy*, and let's memorize one. Write it down and spend the next week memorizing it. Then work it into a conversation. God inspires shouts of pure joy from us. What's your verse? Joy in memorizing it.

#MoreJesusMoreJoy365MemorizingJoy

August 2

"Satisfy us each morning with your unfailing love, so we may sing for joy to the end of our lives." (Psalm 90:14)

Today, let's meet with Jesus in the morning and rest in His loving arms. Something is special about a quiet time with God early in the morning. Meeting Him first-thing before the sun rises and spending time in His unfailing love makes you sing for joy all day long. Try it and tell us how it went. Joy in His morning love.

#MoreJesusMoreJoy365MorningLove

August

3

"He covers the heavens with clouds, provides rain for the earth, and makes the grass grow in mountain pastures." (Psalm 147:8)

Today, think of a time when you really noticed God's landscape. Where were you, and what caught your attention? Maybe you were taking a flight with your head in the clouds, looking down at the patchwork-covered earth. Or maybe you were on a hike, with each step grounded in His creation. Joy in the creation.

#MoreJesusMoreJoy365creation

August

4

"You thrill me, LORD, with all you have done for me! I sing for joy because of what you have done." (Psalm 92:4)

Today, let's proclaim what the Lord's hand has done for us. What has He done for you that makes you sing for joy? Joy comes when we praise God for what He has already done in our lives. Joy in the work of His hands.

#MoreJesusMoreJoy365HisWork

August

5

"Light shines on the godly, and joy on those whose hearts are right." (Psalm 97:11)

Today, let's think of a Jesus follower whose light is easily seen. The person usually has the kind of sparkle in his or her eyes that only God gives. He or she glows and radiates like Moses did from spending time with God. Spending time reading the Bible and praying makes you right with God. The reward is walking in the light that He gives. Share what the Light of God looks like. Joy in His light.

#MoreJesusMoreJoy365HisLight

August

6

"When he prays to God, he will be accepted. And God will receive him with joy and restore him to good standing." (Job 33:26)

Today, let's bring joy to God by praying to Him. It's fun to think that we can bring God joy. He is the Keeper of joy. What is your prayer to Him today? Joy perseveres within when we connect with God and pray to Him. Joy in prayer.

#MoreJesusMoreJoy365prayer

August

7

"Live in harmony with each other. Don't be too proud to enjoy the company of ordinary people. And don't think you know it all!" (Romans 12:16)

Today, let's conduct a harmony check. Do we socialize with all walks of life? Let's look for those starting out in life or struggling and befriend them by offering kind words of encouragement. Sometimes a smile is more powerful than words. How do you live in harmony with others? Joy in the entire community.

#MoreJesusMoreJoy365NoStatusNeeded

August

8

"Deceit fills hearts that are plotting evil; joy fills hearts that are planning peace!" (Proverbs 12:20)

Today, let's look deep into our hearts and search for the places where evil has taken root. Then let's promote peace within ourselves by telling God all about it. Ask Him how to fix it, and let it go. What other ways can you promote peace from within? Joy in being at peace in the world.

#MoreJesusMoreJoy365peace

August 9

"He will once again fill your mouth with laughter and your lips with shouts of joy." (Job 8:21)

Today, let's look back to a time when we couldn't find any laughter. Life is hard. When we are faithful to Jesus, He will return our laughter to us. Listen for laughter today, and join in when you hear it. Jesus rejoices over us and fills our mouths with laughter so we can face each day. What makes you laugh? Joy in laughter.

#MoreJesusMoreJoy365LaughterReturns

August 10

"Keep my commands and you will live; guard my teachings as the apple of your eye." (Proverbs 7:2, NIV)

Today, let's snag an apple to eat. As you bite into its sweetness, be reminded of the sweet joy in following His teachings. Show us the apple of your eye. Joy in cherishing the goodness of God.

#MoreJesusMoreJoy365AppleOfYourEye

August

11

"No eye has seen, no ear has heard, and no mind has imagined what God has prepared for those who love him." (1 Corinthians 2:9)

Today, let's share what God has prepared for those who love Him. Are you walking and living in the gifts He's given you or what is He preparing for you right now? Even though the best is yet to come in Heaven, God still provides for us here. Joy in His preparations.

#MoreJesusMoreJoy365preparations

August

12

"The sun rises at one end of the heavens and follows its course to the other end. Nothing can hide from its heat." (Psalm 19:6)

Today, let's gather some sunflowers. Maybe grab some at the grocery store or look at some online. Sunflowers track the sun. Their "heads" composed of many florets face east in the morning and follow the sun as it sets in the west. Do our heads move and follow the Son of God? Let the sunflower be a reminder to keep our eyes on the Son. Show us your sunflowers. Joy in following the Son.

#MoreJesusMoreJoy365TheSon

August

13

"The LORD himself goes before you and will be with you; he will never leave you nor forsake you. Do not be afraid; do not be discouraged." (Deuteronomy 31:8, NIV)

Today, let's write down a promise from the Bible, then write your response to the scripture. For example, your response to the scripture *"I will never leave you nor forsake you,"* might be, "Lord, I too promise never to leave You nor forsake You." Hold that promise and carry it with you today. Which promise did you find? Joy in knowing His promises.

#MoreJesusMoreJoy365promises

August

14

"Look up into the heavens. Who created all the stars? He brings them out like an army, one after another, calling each by its name. Because of his great power and incomparable strength, not a single one is missing." (Isaiah 40:26)

Today, let's look up and turn your head to the sky every chance you get. Look up from your phone, computer, or book. Did the sky's color change throughout the day? Describe the star filled sky. Joy in His skies.

#MoreJesusMoreJoy365TheSky

August

15

"Taste and see that the LORD is good. Oh, the joys of those who take refuge in him!" (Psalm 34:8)

Today, let's eat the rainbow. Throughout your day, try to incorporate these colors into your meal: red, orange, yellow, green, blue, indigo, and violet. Of course, you can always cheat and grab a red pack of brightly colored candies if you need to. How many colors did you eat? Joy in the savory and tasty love of God.

#MoreJesusMoreJoy365EatTheRainbow

August

16

"The Son radiates God's own glory and expresses the very character of God, and he sustains everything by the mighty power of his command. When he had cleansed us from our sins, he sat down in the place of honor at the right hand of the majestic God in heaven." (Hebrews 1:3)

Today, let's spend time with Jesus and be reminded that we are spending time with God Himself. How will you spend time with Jesus today? Will you read the Bible, pray, confess your sins? Jesus forgives every sin confessed to Him. Get close to God through His Son. Joy in the Son of God.

#MoreJesusMoreJoy365SonOfGod

August
17

"I look up to the mountains—does my help come from there? My help comes from the LORD, who made heaven and earth!" (Psalm 121:1, 2)

Today, let's share some pictures of God's gorgeous mountains to remind us to look up high—to Him. God watches over us and waits for us to look to Him for help. He is always there for us day or night. Keep your head held high and look to Him. Joy in His help.

#MoreJesusMoreJoy365HisHelp

August
18

"I thirst for God, the living God. When can I go and stand before him?" (Psalm 42:2)

Today, let's consider the amount of time you spend with God. Is it enough or do you need to rearrange your schedule? Does your soul thirst for God, and do you anticipate the time you get to spend with Him? The more we know about God, the more we want to know about God. Knowing Him consumes us and becomes our lifeline. Joy in meeting with God.

#MoreJesusMoreJoy365MeetingWithGod

August

19

"But Moses protested to God, 'Who am I to appear before Pharaoh? Who am I to lead the people of Israel out of Egypt?' God answered, 'I will be with you. And this is your sign that I am the one who has sent you: When you have brought the people out of Egypt, you will worship God at this very mountain.'" (Exodus 3:11, 12)

Today, let's not make excuses when God asks us to serve. We often feel inadequate for the job that the Lord asks us to do and don't obey. God is always with us and goes before us. He knows that we can complete any task He assigns. What has He asked you to do that seemed impossible? Joy in serving Him.

#MoreJesusMoreJoy365ServeHim.

August

20

"Restore us, LORD God Almighty; make your face shine on us, that we may be saved." (Psalm 80:19, NIV)

Today, let's take a little break and go outside. Let's throw back our heads and bask in God's ambient glow of sunshine. Rest in it. Breathe it in. Salvation and sunshine are good for the soul. Show us your *Son shine.* Joy in His rays.

#MoreJesusMoreJoy365SonShine

August 21

"Whoever loves a pure heart and gracious speech will have the king as a friend."
(Proverbs 22:11)

Today, let's think back to a time when our speech wasn't gracious. How did the Lord help you change it? The Lord wants us to have gracious speech toward others and how we think and talk to ourselves. If we struggle with our words, we simply need to ask God to help us to be gracious with our speech, and our request will be fulfilled. No foul language, gossip, or slanderous talk anymore as He will remove it from our lips. Joy in being the King's friend.

#MoreJesusMoreJoy365TheKingsFriend

August 22

"Then I said to them: What is this high place you go to?'" (It is called Bamah to this day)."
(Ezekiel 20:29, NIV)

Today, let's look through our Bibles to find some of the most humorous things we've underlined. In Ezekiel, *Bamah* is known as a high place, yet it is also slang for "Alabama." What is the funniest scripture you've read in the Bible and had a joyful laugh over? Joy in funny scripture.

#MoreJesusMoreJoy365JoyfulScripture

August 23

"If your enemies are hungry, give them food to eat. If they are thirsty, give them water to drink. You will heap burning coals of shame on their heads, and the LORD will reward you." (Proverbs 25:21, 22)

Today, let's look at this good versus evil lesson in scripture. Hating evil is acceptable, but we are still called to love, do good, and to pray for our enemies. What are some prayers we can pray over our enemies? Jesus is the Judge, and He is the One who will do our avenging. We can take our hurts and pains caused by others straight to Him. We give all trust to Jesus when we repay evil with good. Joy in trusting the Judge.

#MoreJesusMoreJoy365LoveWins

August 24

"Let all that I am praise the LORD; may I never forget the good things he does for me." (Psalm 103:2)

Today, let's count and number our blessings and write them down. Maybe use a new pack of sticky notes and spread your joy blessings all around your home. Do you have 365 blessings—one for each day of the year? How many did you realize and which ones were new blessings? Joy in His blessings. #MoreJesusMoreJoy365blessings

August

25

"In his kindness God called you to share in his eternal glory by means of Christ Jesus. So after you have suffered a little while, he will restore, support, and strengthen you, and he will place you on a firm foundation." (1 Peter 5:10)

Today, let's look at the suffering we face here on earth. Out of our difficult times, miracles can happen. God doesn't let any circumstance go to waste. He creates beauty from dust. What beauty has He created from your dust? We are also reminded there is no suffering in Heaven. Joy in the dust.

#MoreJesusMoreJoy365BeautyFromDust

August

26

"Therefore, go and make disciples of all the nations, baptizing them in the name of the Father and the Son and the Holy Spirit." (Matthew 28:19)

Today, let's share about baptism. When were you baptized or have you seen a baptism? *Baptism* with water is "an outward expression of an inward feeling." Watching baptism is a joyous event, with hands clapping as another believer expressing his or her love for Jesus. Joy in baptism.

#MoreJesusMoreJoy365baptism

August 27

"Jesus looked at them and said, 'With man this is impossible, but with God all things are possible.'" (Matthew 19:26)

Today, let's look at the many times we have lived out this scripture. What has God asked you to do that you just knew was impossible, but you were able to accomplish? If He asks us to do something, He makes it possible for us to complete the task in His power. When we think we can't keep going or do the impossible, we go further and complete it. With Him, nothing is impossible. Joy in mission impossible.

#MoreJesusMoreJoy365MissionImpossible

August 28

"He will cover you with his feathers. He will shelter you with his wings. His faithful promises are your armor and protection." (Psalm 91:4)

Today, let's look at our awesome Protector, God! He provides, protects, and guides us through all of our trials and fears. Take in the imagery of God's covering us with His feathers. What does this look like to you? Joy in the great Protector.

#MoreJesusMoreJoy365protector

August

29

"For I have given rest to the weary and joy to the sorrowing." (Jeremiah 31:25)

Today, let's let our smile and love for Jesus change the world, but we must be careful not to let the world change our smile and love for Him. Don't let the world change your smile by plugging back into God daily by reading His Word, praying, and spending time with Him. Let Him give rest and restore what the world has taken from you. Now show us what you look like smiling, shining, and showing the love of God. Joy in being His light.

#MoreJesusMoreJoy365CarryTheLight

August

30

"So encourage each other and build each other up, just as you are already doing." (1 Thessalonians 5:11)

Today, let's acknowledge and appreciate those working around us. Consider writing a note of thanks to your mail carrier and leave it in your mailbox. Or write a thank you to the one who delivers your work mail. Let these people know you see them working in all seasons and how you appreciate all of the letters and packages that they diligently deliver. Joy in appreciating others.

#MoreJesusMoreJoy365appreciate

August

31

"One thing I ask from the LORD, this only do I seek: that I may dwell in the house of the LORD all the days of my life, to gaze on the beauty of the LORD and to seek him in his temple." (Psalm 27:4, NIV)

Today, let's consider one thing to ask from the Lord. What is it? What is the joy of your heart? What is the one thing you want to ask so badly but you haven't? It is an honor and a great joy to seek Him in prayer. Joy in dwelling in the house of the Lord.

#MoreJesusMoreJoy365OneThing

September

1

"Work willingly at whatever you do, as though you were working for the Lord rather than for people." (Colossians 3:23)

Today, let's be reminded that whatever task we're given in the workplace or in the home that we can find joy in because we are working for the Lord. Work at it with all your heart because you're working for Him. Give Him your best. On what are you working for the Lord? Joy in working for the Lord.

#MoreJesusMoreJoy365Working

September 2

"May my meditation be pleasing to him, as I rejoice in the LORD." (Psalm 104:34, NIV).

Today, let's search the Bible for a piece of scripture about which you would like to have a better understanding. Write it out, carry it with you, and contemplate it throughout the day. Have it on a loop in the background, running through your mind. You can also practice saying it out loud. At the end of the day, jot down a few notes that God taught you about it. What's your verse, and what did you learn? Joy in meditating on His Word.

#MoreJesusMoreJoy365meditating

September 3

"The LORD says, 'I will rescue those who love me. I will protect those who trust in my name.'" (Psalm 91:14)

Today, let's acknowledge the Lord's great name and His protection over us. Write a prayer thanking Jesus for the daily protections that He provides because we trust in Him. Joy in protection.

#MoreJesusMoreJoy365HeProtects

September 4

"Cast your cares on the LORD and he will sustain you; he will never let the righteous be shaken." (Psalm 55:22, NIV)

Today, let's search our hearts to see if we are still holding onto something we should cast off to the Lord. What is it? It is a job promotion or a to-do list? Let's quickly hand it over to Jesus. He wants us to hand our hurts, pains, and worries to Him so we can let go and be at peace. Joy in casting our cares to the Lord.

#MoreJesusMoreJoy365CastYourCares

September 5

"I love the Lord because he hears my voice and my prayer for mercy. Because he bends down to listen, I will pray as long as I have breath!" (Psalm 116:1, 2)

Today, let's practice mindful breathing. Take in a few deep breaths before we pray. As we do, recognize God is always listening. He can hear our quietest, silent prayers to Him. What are your prayers today? As long as we have breath, let's pray to Him. Joy in praying to Him.

#MoreJesusMoreJoy365pray

September

6

"Stay alert! Watch out for your great enemy, the devil. He prowls around like a roaring lion, looking for someone to devour. Stand firm against him, and be strong in your faith. Remember that your family of believers all over the world is going through the same kind of suffering you are." (1 Peter 5:8, 9)

Today, let's make a public statement that Satan is not allowed in our life. There is no room for him in our life—only Jesus. With a marker, write *"Not Today Satan"* on the bottom of your shoes. Declare your victory with each step you take. Joy in resisting evil.

#MoreJesusMoreJoy365NotTodaySatan

September

7

"Humble yourselves before the Lord, and he will lift you up in honor." (James 4:10)

Today, let's define what it means to be humble. The Bible says that when we humble ourselves to God, we submit our weaknesses, ask for His help, and gain His strength. Do you consider yourself a humble being? How are you humble? Joy in being humble.

#MoreJesusMoreJoy365humble

September

8

"It is the LORD who provides the sun to light the day and the moon and stars to light the night, and who stirs the sea into roaring waves. His name is the LORD of Heaven's Armies, and this is what he says." (Jeremiah 31:35)

Today, consider the sunshine, the moon and the stars, and the great big ocean—Jesus has power over it all. Which of the domains that the Lord rules over is your favorite? Joy in an awesome God.

#MoreJesusMoreJoy365AwesomeGod

September

9

"The LORD is compassionate and gracious, slow to anger, abounding in love." (Psalm 103:8, NIV)

Today, let's wholeheartedly praise God for being slow to anger. Let's face it; we mess up every day, and yet every day He forgives our confessed sins to Him. Pause and praise in admiration of His abounding love for you. What does gratitude for His love look like to you? Joy in His abounding love.

#MoreJesusMoreJoy365HisLove

September 10

"May we shout for joy when we hear of your victory and raise a victory banner in the name of our God. May the LORD answer all your prayers." (Psalm 20:5)

Today, let's lift it up and raise a victory banner praising the Lord for answered prayers. How joyous it is when we hear of others' victories. Often our prayers are answered, and raising a banner of praise to the Lord acknowledges His response. What is on your banner? Joy in sharing it with others.

#MoreJesusMoreJoy365victory

September 11

"So they camped or traveled at the LORD's command, and they did whatever the LORD told them through Moses." (Numbers 9:23)

Today, take a good long look at where God has placed you and ask Him what He wants you to do in this place. What place are you in? Trust that God has you right where He wants you to be. Dig in, be present, and find purpose through Him in that place until He commands you to move on. Joy in your current place.

#MoreJesusMoreJoy365ThisPlace

September 12

"Do not listen to them. The LORD your God is testing you to see if you truly love him with all your heart and soul." (Deuteronomy 13:3)

Today, let's start checking everything we hear against the Bible to determine its truth. Modern-day deceivers and false prophets walk among us. We must know our Bibles and study them. When in conversation with others, watching TV, attending church, or listening to an online sermon, be sure to recognize the truth before accepting the teaching. Don't merely hear the truth; scour the Bible for answers, and don't stop until you find them. For what answers have you searched the Bible lately? Joy in being a fact checker.

#MoreJesusMoreJoy365FactChecker

September 13

"Commit yourself to instruction; listen carefully to words of knowledge." (Proverbs 23:12)

Today, let's read the Bible for twenty minutes. Set a timer if you need to and start reading in a place you want. What did you read and what did you learn? Joy in the commitment of knowledge.

#MoreJesusMoreJoy365knowledge

September

14

"A man who makes a vow to the Lord or makes a pledge under oath must never break it. He must do exactly what he said he would do." (Numbers 30:2)

Today, let's think of a promise you kept and one you didn't. The one you kept brought you joy for keeping your word to another, but the promise you didn't keep probably make you feel badly because you let God or others down. How do you feel when others keep their promises? Joy in keeping promises.

#MoreJesusMoreJoy365KeepingPromises

September

15

"Hatred stirs up quarrels, but love makes up for all offenses." (Proverbs 10:12)

Today, let's take a look at how love operates. Sometimes, loving others is not easy, but when we do love and especially show undeserved love, all evil is crushed. Evil cannot stand against our love because God is pure love. How can you show love when it's unexpected? Joy in love.

#MoreJesusMoreJoy365love

September 16

"You should clothe yourselves instead with the beauty that comes from within, the unfading beauty of a gentle and quiet spirit, which is so precious to God." (1 Peter 3:4)

Today, let's consider this scripture. Does it take your breath away? True beauty from the inside out is breathtaking. Which scriptures take away your breath and stop you in your tracks? What do you read in the Bible that brings joy to your heart and makes you smile? Joy in being breathless.

#MoreJesusMoreJoy365BreathlessScripture

September 17

"If you search for good, you will find favor; but if you search for evil, it will find you!" (Proverbs 11:27)

Today, let's look for the good in everyone we meet. Finding the bad traits, faults, and evil in people is easy, but you can choose to be the one who finds the beauty and goodness. What ways can we look for the goodness in people? Be the one who finds the beauty, and then you will find favor. Joy in the beauty of goodness.

#MoreJesusMoreJoy365FindTheBeauty

September

18

"What a blessing it will be to attend a banquet in the Kingdom of God!" (Luke 14:15)

Today, let's take our imaginary, for-now seat at God's table at the banquet in Heaven. We're sitting there with the believers who stood firm until the end, and now we can talk with Jesus face to face. What questions would you like to ask Him? Perhaps your questions include: why do pets have such short life spans, and why don't we get to keep them longer? Maybe you want to ask Him to recap the tower of Babel and how He created all the languages of the world. Joy in heavenly answers.

#MoreJesusMoreJoy365HeavenlyTableTalk

September

19

"But blessed are those who trust in the LORD and have made the LORD their hope and confidence." (Jeremiah 17:7)

Today, let's look at how we trust the Lord. When we trust and believe in the Lord, His strength becomes our strength. Do you believe He can do what He says? What ways can we trust Him? Joy in trust.

#MoreJesusMoreJoy365trust

September

20

"For the Lamb on the throne will be their Shepherd. He will lead them to springs of life-giving water. And God will wipe every tear from their eyes." (Revelation 7:17)

Today, let's take comfort in knowing that one day we will cry no more tears. In our eternal home, all of our needs will be met perfectly with no more sin and no more pain. No more tears will be shed. We will be Home. How does this eternal comfort make you feel while you're here? Joy in going home.

#MoreJesusMoreJoy365GoingHome

September

21

"Your word is a lamp to guide my feet and a light for my path." (Psalm 119:105)

Today, let's envision our feet planted firmly in God's Word. His Word is our light that shines in our path and guides us so we do not stumble. Life is full of obstacles. Which words of God keeps you the most grounded? Joy in being grounded in His Word.

#MoreJesusMoreJoy365grounded

September

22

"For everything there is a season, a time for every activity under heaven." (Ecclesiastes 3:1)

Today, let's change with the seasons, and change one of your passwords to include something about Jesus. This new password could be your favorite Bible verse or a character trait of Jesus. As we change with the seasons of life, let's keep Jesus with us every day. Which account did you change? Joy in every season of life with Jesus.

#MoreJesusMoreJoy365SeasonsChange

September

23

"For everyone has sinned; we all fall short of God's glorious standard." (Romans 3:23)

Today, let's look for the color *black*, which represents our sin. We all sin and try to do better each day. Let's ask God for a clean heart and forgiveness of any sins that we have committed. Let's wear, eat, or draw something with black and be reminded that Jesus forgives us even while were sinners. Joy in being loved right where you are at.

#MoreJesusMoreJoy365LovedToday

September

24

"For this is how God loved the world: He gave his one and only Son, so that everyone who believes in him will not perish but have eternal life." (John 3:16)

Today, let's look for the color *blue*, which represents the hope that we have in Jesus. Let's wear something blue today and share this truth with others as you are able. This hope that we have is in God who loves us so much He sent His One and only Son to redeem us from our sins and reconcile us back to God. Jesus came to take away our sins so that we may be acceptable to God again. Joy in hopeful reconciliation.

#MoreJesusMoreJoy365reconciled

September

25

"For the wages of sin is death, but the free gift of God is eternal life through Christ Jesus our Lord." (Romans 6:23)

Today, let's look for the color *red*, which represents Jesus' blood shed for our sins. Show us the red you see today. Be on the lookout for it, take note of it, and smile in remembrance of what Jesus did for us on the cross. Jesus offered Himself as the payment for our sins so that we may have eternal life. Joy in the color red!

#MoreJesusMoreJoy365red

September 26

"'Come now, let's settle this,' says the LORD. 'Though your sins are like scarlet, I will make them as white as snow. Though they are red like crimson, I will make them as white as wool.'"
(Isaiah 1:18)

Today, let's look for the color *white* and be reminded that our sins are washed white by Jesus. We believers are no longer black as sin, He shed His blood for us and we are now made clean and white as snow. Show us something white that reminds you of how He made you clean. Joy in being made clean.

#MoreJesusMoreJoy365IAmClean

September 27

"They replied, 'Believe in the Lord Jesus and you will be saved, along with everyone in your household.'" (Acts 16:31)

Today, let's look for the color *orange*, which reminds us that we are saved and safe. Orange is a safety color that represents protection and makes you aware of its presence. Show us your best safety orange today. When we believe in Jesus, we are safe in Him and saved through Him. Joy in His safety.

#MoreJesusMoreJoy365safety

September

28

"This means that anyone who belongs to Christ has become a new person. The old life is gone; a new life has begun!" (2 Corinthians 5:17)

Today, let's look for *green*, which represents our new life in Jesus. When we accept and trust in Jesus, He makes us a completely new creation, and we have a new beginning each day. Show us your new life-green color today, it could be your green shirt or a new green plant. Joy in being a new creation.

#MoreJesusMorJoy365NewCreation

September

29

"You love him even though you have never seen him. Though you do not see him now, you trust him; and you rejoice with a glorious, inexpressible joy." (1 Peter 1:8)

Today, let's look for the color *yellow,* which represents the joy we have found in Jesus. Though we don't see Him, we believe in Him and are full of inexpressible joy for Him. The fact that we believe without seeing Him makes Jesus the most important priority in this life. Show us your best joy-filled yellow. Joy in believing without seeing.

#MoreJesusMoreJoy365believe

September

30

"I give them eternal life, and they will never perish. No one can snatch them away from me."
(John 10:28)

Today, let's look for the color *gold*, which represents eternal life with Jesus. We believers who trust in Jesus will never perish and thanks to Him we will meet Him face-to-face in Heaven. One day we will wear the gold crown given to us in eternity. Joy in eternal life.

#MoreJesusMoreJoy365EternalLife

October

1

"O LORD, if you heal me, I will be truly healed; if you save me, I will be truly saved. My praises are for you alone!" (Jeremiah 17:14)

Today, let's look at how God heals and saves us. From what has He saved you? How has He healed you? Have you praised Him for His compassion? We must never stop praising the goodness and the healing of God. Joy in a healed soul.

#MoreJesusMoreJoy365HealedSoul

October

2

"The LORD will work out his plans for my life—
for your faithful love, O LORD, endures forever.
Don't abandon me, for you made me." (Psalm
138:8)

Today, let's be reminded that the Lord has mighty plans for
our lives, and we need to include Him in our plans. God
created each one of us with a specific plan in mind. Have you
discovered His plan for your life? Joy in His plans.

#MoreJesusMoreJoy365HisPlans

October

3

"But as for me, I know that my Redeemer lives,
and he will stand upon the earth at last." (Job
19:25)

Today, let's consider the strong foundation of faith that Job
had in God. Job was a man who had everything—family,
wealth, and good health. Because God trusted Job, he lost it
all, except his faith in God. How do you fare when testing
comes? How do we get a strong foundation of faith like Job,
who still praised God through it all? Joy in unshakeable faith.

#MoreJesusMoreJoy365UnshakeableFaith

October

4

"Then David continued, 'Be strong and courageous, and do the work. Don't be afraid or discouraged, for the LORD God, my God, is with you. He will not fail you or forsake you. He will see to it that all the work related to the Temple of the LORD is finished correctly.'" (2 Chronicles 28:20)

Today, let's see how Solomon was overwhelmed with the task God had given Him to build the enormous temple for the Lord. His father reminded him to be strong and courageous and with God's help, he would not fail. What has the Lord asked you to do that made you almost freeze in your tracks with fear? How did you complete the task? Joy in an unfailing God.

#MoreJesusMoreJoy365UnfailingGod

October

5

"For this, O LORD, I will praise you among the nations; I will sing praises to your name." (Psalm 18:49)

Today, let's praise Him with all we've got. Sometimes it's a boisterous dance party, and sometimes it's a silent prayer. Whatever you've got today, choose to praise Him with it. How will you praise the Lord on this day? Joy in choosing to praise Jesus. #MoreJesusMoreJoy365PraiseHim

October

6

"So the Lord scattered them from there over all the earth, and they stopped building the city. That is why it was called Babel—because there the LORD confused the language of the whole world. From there the LORD scattered them over the face of the whole earth." (Genesis 11: 8, 9, NIV)

Today, let's just think about the Lord's creating all the languages of the world and scattering the people all over the face of the earth. God's people originally had one language, but the people were working together to build a tower—a shrine to themselves. As a result, the Lord confused the people and scattered them. Today, we are still trying to learn how to work together as a people of different languages and cultures. Share a friend of a different culture or language and the joys you have trying to communicate. Joy in confusion.

#MoreJesusMoreJoy365confusion

October

7

"Blessed are those who listen to me, watching daily at my doors, waiting at my doorway." (Proverbs 8:34, NIV)

Today, let's be mindful of each doorway you walk through, remembering your commitment to Jesus. Each door we walk through is one door closer to the last one. Show us your vision of Heaven's door. Joy in commitment.

#MoreJesusMoreJoy365commitment

October 8

"When he received honor and glory from God the Father. The voice from the majestic glory of God said to him, 'This is my dearly loved Son, who brings me great joy.'" (2 Peter 1:17)

Today, we too are thankful for the obedience of Jesus. He who pleased His Father also pleased us from following the will of God for His life's purpose. How are you being obedient to God for your life's purpose? Joy in honoring Jesus.

#MoreJesusMoreJoy365LifesPurpose

October 9

"Take your son, your only son—yes, Isaac, whom you love so much—and go to the land of Moriah. Go and sacrifice him as a burnt offering on one of the mountains, which I will show you." (Genesis 22:2)

Today, let's consider Abraham's obedience to God. After Abraham prepared his beloved son for sacrifice as the Lord had instructed, God sent an angel to cancel the request. God had seen His friend's obedience. What has God asked you to modern-day sacrifice and then cancelled the request? Did He want to see if you would do it for Him? How did you handle this difficult request? Joy in obedience.

#MoreJesusMoreJoy365obedience

October

10

"For that is what God is like. He is our God forever and ever, and he will guide us until we die." (Psalm 48:14)

Today, let's look at how God takes care of everything. He's even given us an Owner's Manual with instructions on how to live—the Bible, and a Guide—the Holy Spirit to navigate. We all came with an Instruction Manual. God uses this very tool to speak to us. Share with us your favorite part about your Bible. Joy in having an Owner's Manual.

#MoreJesusMoreJoy365OwnersManual

October

11

"For God is not unjust. He will not forget how hard you have worked for him and how you have shown your love to him by caring for other believers, as you still do." (Hebrews 6:10)

Today, let's thank those serving missions, military, law enforcement, first responders, and those serving weekly in our churches. Share a prayer request for one who helps and shows love for others. Serving one another as Jesus asked is worthy of our praise. Joy in service.

#MoreJesusMoreJoy365service

October

12

"Do not store up for yourselves treasures on earth, where moths and vermin destroy, and where thieves break in and steal. But store up for yourselves treasures in heaven, where moths and vermin do not destroy, and where thieves do not break in and steal. For where your treasure is, there your heart will be also." (Matthew 6:19-21)

Today, let's store up some treasures in Heaven. Sock 'em away like a squirrel stores nuts. These deeds that we do, such as tithing or helping others, are unseen by others. We don't receive a thank you or tell others about them. Often only those receiving the treasure (the recipients) know about it. What are other ways to store up treasures in Heaven? Joy in treasures in heaven.

#MoreJesusMoreJoy365TreasuresInHeaven

October

13

"For the word of God will never fail." (Luke 1:37)

Today, let's consider how our faith has helped us through life's trials. Whatever you have going on in your life or if you are in need of direction, you can search the Bible for answers and ask God to help. The Word of God will never fail you, and nothing is impossible with God. Share how your faith in the Word of God has helped you. Joy in a never-failing God.

#MoreJesusMoreJoy365NeverFails

October

14

"Jesus called a little child to him and put the child among them. Then he said, "I tell you the truth, unless you turn from your sins and become like little children, you will never get into the Kingdom of Heaven." (Matthew 18:2, 3)

Today, let's connect with our inner child and *skip* somewhere. That somewhere may be from the grocery store to your car or from your office to the conference room. Just *Skip to My Lou* for you! If you already do these things, you may *skip* this exercise. Oh, and ladies, make sure you have a purse that zips today. Joy in a childlike faith.

#MoreJesusMoreJoy365ChildlikeFaith

October

15

"But each day the LORD pours his unfailing love upon me, and through each night I sing his songs, praying to God who gives me life." (Psalm 42:8)

Today, let's receive through prayer, all of God's unfailing love. He can't wait until we come to Him, thanking and asking Him in prayer. How did He pour His unfailing love upon you when you prayed your heart out to Him? What does unfailing love look like? Joy in His unfailing love.

#MoreJesusMoreJoy365UnfailingLove

October

16

"Yours, O LORD, is the greatness, the power, the glory, the victory, and the majesty. Everything in the heavens and on earth is yours, O LORD, and this is your kingdom. We adore you as the one who is over all things." (1 Chronicles 29:11)

Today, let's celebrate Boss Appreciation Day. Smile and cultivate joy in our hearts, in the workplace, in the home office, or in your household. Take heart and smile because you know who your Boss really is. Write your boss a letter of appreciation and share it with us. Joy in Jesus as head of the kingdom.

#MoreJesusMoreJoy365JesusIsMyBoss

October

17

"Yes, joyful are those who live like this! Joyful indeed are those whose God is the LORD." (Psalm 144:15)

Today, let's consider these words that David wrote. He wrote this psalm about rejoicing always because we are in God's care. Whether we are praising Him for blessings or crying out to Him in times of trouble, joyful are we because He is our Lord. Are you joyfully resting in God's care? How is He caring for you today? Joy in His care.

#MoreJesusMoreJoy365HisCare

October

18

"When you go through deep waters, I will be with you. When you go through rivers of difficulty, you will not drown. When you walk through the fire of oppression, you will not be burned up; the flames will not consume you." (Isaiah 43:2)

Today, let's take the time to write a thank-you note to the nearest fire company. Thank the firefighters for the safety and their service in your community. They support the community in the most difficult of times and are often volunteers. Pray for God to protect those He sent for our safety. Where is your local fire company? Joy in knowing helping hands are waiting.

#MoreJesusMoreJoy365HelpingHands

October

19

"This is good and pleases God our Savior, who wants everyone to be saved and to understand the truth." (1 Timothy 2:3, 4)

Today, let's search our hearts for someone whom God wants to hear the truth. Pray and reach out to them as the Spirit leads. Maybe it's a visit, a phone call, a note, or a text. Or maybe it's an invitation for coffee or lunch. How will you reach out? Joy in sharing the truth.

#MoreJesusMoreJoy365ShareTheTruth

October
20

"This is what the Lord says—your Redeemer, the Holy One of Israel: 'I am the LORD your God, who teaches you what is good for you and leads you along the paths you should follow.'"
(Isaiah 48:17)

Today, consider if an area of your life needs God's guidance. In prayer, ask Jesus to direct in a renewal of that area of your life. Whether it's a subject matter or an area of friendship, He will teach you the way to go. What does His path look like for you today? Joy in His path.

#MoreJesusMoreJoy365HisPath

October
21

"Let your conversation be gracious and attractive so that you will have the right response for everyone." (Colossians 4:6)

Today, let's not let one ungracious word roll off of our tongue. Bite it if you have to. What are some gracious words you would like to hear? Maybe it's positive and uplifting speech instead of dumping on others with complaints. Keep kindness in your words. Joy in being gracious.

#MoreJesusMoreJoy365GraciousSpeech

October

22

"I could have no greater joy than to hear that my children are following the truth." (3 John 4)

Today, let's be on the lookout for those whom God has placed in your life to hear and see the truth. Maybe it's your friend's child or one you taught in Sunday school or one you mentored or volunteered to help. It takes a village to teach a child; it's everyone's responsibility to set good examples and point our youth to the truth of Jesus. How many do you know are now following the truth? Count them down and celebrate! Joy in the truth.

#MoreJesusMoreJoy365truth

October

23

"So letting your sinful nature control your mind leads to death. But letting the Spirit control your mind leads to life and peace." (Romans 8:6)

Today, let's remember how joyful it is to have the best of guides—the Holy Spirit. The Spirit is our guide through life, gently tugging, correcting, and uplifting us. How do you let the Spirit guide you and bring you peace? Joy in a good guide.

#MoreJesusMoreJoy365GoodGuide

October

24

"Come, let us worship and bow down. Let us kneel before the LORD our maker, for he is our God. We are the people he watches over, the flock under his care. If only you would listen to his voice today!" (Psalm 95: 6, 7)

Today, let's kneel before Jesus. When was the last time you took to your knees and prayed to Jesus? Oftentimes, we fall to our knees when we are suffering through trials and experiencing tragedy. Let's try to kneel before God today and offer up praises for the things He's already done for us. Maybe it's a new practice of kneeling by your bed to say your prayers. Joy in kneeling before the Lord.

#MoreJesusMoreJoy365KneelBeforeHim

October

25

"He heals the brokenhearted and bandages their wounds." (Psalm 147:3)

Today, let's remember to come to Him with any and every heartache we have. After all, He is the only One who can take away our pain. He makes us new again and complete. He mends our cracked hearts and bodies with His love. Show us your mended heart from Jesus. Joy in being mended by Him.

#MoreJesusMoreJoy365mended

October 26

"And yet, O LORD, you are our Father. We are the clay, and you are the potter. We all are formed by your hand." (Isaiah 64:8)

Today, let's think back to the first time when you allowed yourself to be molded by God. If you were a piece of clay, what would you look like in the Potter's hand? How has He molded you? What one word comes to mind as you consider this question? Joy in being molded by the Potter's hand.

#MoreJesusMoreJoy365molded

October 27

"So don't be afraid; you are more valuable to God than a whole flock of sparrows." (Matthew 10:31)

Today, let's gaze out a window, and be on the lookout for birds. God knows everything that happens—even to the sparrows. You are valued and worth more than many sparrows! Each time you see one throughout your day, smile big knowing your worth in God. How many birds did you see? Joy in worthiness.

#MoreJesusMoreJoy365valuable

October

28

"Wait patiently for the LORD. Be brave and courageous. Yes, wait patiently for the LORD."
(Psalm 27:14)

Today, let's look at why we wait on the Lord. Waiting is hard, but Jesus is worth our wait. God's timing is more than perfect. During the wait, He grows, shapes, and strengthens us. We wait on Him because we're often not ready for what He is going to give us. When He deems us ready, we find the waiting is so worthwhile. For what have you waited on the Lord? How did He bless you in His timing? Joy in waiting for the Lord.

#MoreJesusMoreJoy365PatientlyWaiting

October

29

"Then I heard the Lord asking, "Whom should I send as a messenger to this people? Who will go for us?" I said, "Here I am. Send me." (Isaiah 6:8)

Today, let's be aware of God's will and be ready to say, "Here I am; send me." Seemingly no braver words can be uttered by man; yet if we don't go, His will in our lives will never be done. Have you ever said to God, "Here I am, Lord; send me"? How did He use you? Joy in being sent.

#MoreJesusMoreJoy365SendMe

October

30

"No, O people, the LORD has told you what is good, and this is what he requires of you: to do what is right, to love mercy, and to walk humbly with your God." (Micah 6:8)

Today, let's examine our relationship with God to determine where we need to be humbled and write it down. How are we treating others and ourselves? Where in your life are you not waiting on God's guidance? Joy in being humbled.

#MoreJesusMoreJoy365humbled

October

31

"He said to his disciples, 'The harvest is great, but the workers are few.'" (Matthew 9:37)

Today, let's look around us at the harvest. The hues of the earth have changed, the air has cooled, and the time is ripe for the picking. Who around you could you invite to work for Jesus? People often simply need to know how or be shown how to work. What is your prayer today for the harvest? Joy in the harvest.

#MoreJesusMoreJoy365harvest

November

1

"Let the message about Christ, in all its richness, fill your lives. Teach and counsel each other with all the wisdom he gives. Sing psalms and hymns and spiritual songs to God with thankful hearts." (Colossians 3:16)

Today, write out your favorite scripture. If you have several, pick the one that is speaking to your heart. Carry it in your pocket and work it into a conversation when you can or when the Holy Spirit provides. Share your verse with us too. Joy in sharing the good news.

#MoreJesusMoreJoy365GoodNews

November

2

"I stand at the door and knock. If you hear my voice and open the door, I will come in, and we will share a meal together as friends." (Revelation 3:20)

Today, let's set a place for the Lord at our dinner table. Of course, He wouldn't need any food on His plate, but setting the place will add pure joy to your ambience. If dining alone, all the better time for a chat with Him. Show us your table setting for the King. Joy in knowing God is always with us.

#MoreJesusMoreJoy365DineWithTheKing

November

3

"Always be prepared to give an answer to everyone who asks you to give the reason for the hope that you have. But do this with gentleness and respect." (1 Peter 3:15, NIV)

Today, let's get prepared to give an answer for the hope we have in Jesus. As believers, others want to know why we love Jesus. Let's prayerfully consider our go-to response. Maybe you serve so others can see who Jesus is and feel His love through you. Or maybe you have scripture memorized when someone asks about your love for Jesus. What's your reason for the hope you have? Joy in being prepared.

#MoreJesusMoreJoy365ReasonForMyHope

November

4

"For my Father has given them to me, and he is more powerful than anyone else. No one can snatch them from the Father's hand." (John 10:29)

Today, let's declare that we are in God's hand and mentally place our hand in His. No one and nothing will snatch us out of His hand. What does it look like when your hand is placed in His? Is His hand giant-sized compared to yours? Joy in being His.

#MoreJesusMoreJoy365HisHand

November

5

"But encourage one another daily, as long as it is called 'Today,' so that none of you may be hardened by sin's deceitfulness." (Hebrews 3:13, NIV)

Today, let's encourage another believer. Prayerfully consider who to reach out to, then text, phone, or write the person a note. You could tell this person to keep on keeping on and that you're praying for him or her. What are your encouraging words to other believers today? Share your advice with us. Joy in encouraging others.

#MoreJesusMoreJoy365encourage

November

6

"She is more precious than rubies; nothing you desire can compare with her." (Proverbs 3:15, NIV)

Today, let's put on our finest or favorite jewelry. Doesn't matter if it's not fancy—as long as you love it. Get out the pearls you always save for a special occasion or those cuff links and a fancy watch. Or even a special pin someone gave you. Be fabulous, be fancy, and be reminded you are far more precious than rubies. Joy in being valued.

#MoreJesusMorejoy365valued

November 7

"O LORD, you have examined my heart and know everything about me. You know when I sit down or stand up. You know my thoughts even when I'm far away." (Psalm 139:1, 2)

Today, let's have Jesus on our mind with whatever task we are doing. Have conversations with Him throughout the day. While making dinner, give Him a recap of your day. While waiting at the checkout, thank Him for everything He's done for you so far this day. Or praise Him for someone else. Where did He go with you today? Joy in having Jesus on your mind.

#MoreJesusMoreJoy365JesusMinded

November 8

"A single day in your courts is better than a thousand anywhere else! I would rather be a gatekeeper in the house of my God than live the good life in the homes of the wicked." (Psalm 84:10)

Today, tell us how many days you have spent elsewhere. Too many to count? The days you've spent in His courts make the unruly days fade. If you would rather be a gatekeeper in the house of the Lord than live with the wicked, declare this scripture today as your own declaration. Joy in the house of the Lord.

#MoreJesusMoreJoy365HisHouse

November

9

"Children are a gift from the LORD; they are a reward from him." (Psalm 127:3)

Today, let's write out this truth in scripture and take a couple copies with you. Mindfully search for families with babies or young children in your surroundings. Share this truth with parents or moms- and dads-to-be. Brighten their day with joy and the truth that children are a gift and a blessing from the Lord. Show us your scriptural truth or share about who you were able to meet. Joy in gifts from the Lord.

#MoreJesusMoreJoy365ChildrenAreGifts

November

10

"Do not be anxious about anything, but in every situation, by prayer and petition, with thanksgiving, present your requests to God." (Philippians 4:6, NIV)

Today, let's turn our worries into prayers and present them to God. Each time you feel anxious, pause and pray, then let it go. He has it; He hears you and is working all things for your good because He loves you. Show us your prayers. Praying publically allows others to join you and petition God on your behalf. Joy in letting your worries go.

#MoreJesusMoreJoy365WorryFree

November

11

"We know what real love is because Jesus gave up his life for us. So we also ought to give up our lives for our brothers and sisters." (1 John 3:16)

Today, let's wear our cross as a reminder that Jesus laid down His life for us. Put on your cross necklace, bracelet, pin, or pocket cross. Draw a cross and place it in your pocket. There is no greater joy than knowing Jesus chose to die for us so that we may live for Him serving others. Love is the cross; show us yours. Joy in the extravagant love of Jesus.

#MoreJesusMoreJoy365JesusLoves

November

12

"Always be joyful. Never stop praying. Be thankful in all circumstances, for this is God's will for you who belong to Christ Jesus." (1 Thessalonians 5:16-18)

Today, let's go to Jesus in prayer 365 times. Yep, that's right—365! Let's pray to Him for all of our needs throughout the morning, thanking and asking Him. Let's pray down the list of our family's needs in the afternoon, and in the evening, bring all of your friends' needs before Him. Keep track with pen and paper to see how many you can do. Joy in constant communion with Jesus.   #MoreJesusMoreJoy365commune

November

13

"I know how to live on almost nothing or with everything. I have learned the secret of living in every situation, whether it is with a full stomach or empty, with plenty or little." (Philippians 4:12)

Today, let's think of our last meal or our last purchase. Was it enough or did we want more? Being content in any situation is drawing on Jesus' strength and His promises to us. Joy is not based on our circumstances and situations; it's based on our ability to be thankful. For what are you thankful? Joy is a choice. Joy in this moment.

#MoreJesusMorejoy365ThisMoment

November

14

"For you have been born again, but not to a life that will quickly end. Your new life will last forever because it comes from the eternal, living word of God." (1 Peter 1:23)

Today, let's show our love for God's Word and share pictures of our Bibles. I know our life's work is contained within its pages—highlighted, underlined, drawn in, coffee-stained, tear-stained—yet still the most beautiful possession we own. Joy in His Word.

#MoreJesusMoreJoy365HisWord

November

15

"But to all who believed him and accepted him, he gave the right to become children of God."
(John 1:12)

Today, we're putting it on again! Place that real or imaginary crown on top of your head. Go ahead; we'll wait. Now pull your shoulders back, straighten your frame and smile your biggest. Let your cheeks show your rosiest glow as your eyes, full of love for Jesus, twinkle. Pure royalty you are! Share a selfie with the title *"Child of God."* Joy in being chosen.

#MoreJesusMoreJoy365chosen

November

16

"Let your roots grow down into him, and let your lives be built on him. Then your faith will grow strong in the truth you were taught, and you will overflow with thankfulness."
(Colossians 2:7)

Today, let's dig deeper and cultivate our souls. Let's grab our Bibles and learn something new. What have you always wondered about but never took the time to look up or study? Is it the purpose of angels or why we tithe? Just turn to the index of your Bible with your subject and explore the Bible for answers. Joy is rooted in the truth.

#MoreJesusMoreJoy365roots

November

17

"Let all that I am praise the LORD; with my whole heart, I will praise his holy name." (Psalm 103:1)

Today, let's praise God with our whole heart, glorious mind, and soul. In this psalm David is praising God with everything fiber of his being, listing every blessing God has ever given him. His overwhelming gratitude welled up in his soul. When we are running low on energy, we merely need to think of every blessing the Lord has given us, and the gratitude will fill our tank back up to full or overflowing. What was the last blessing the Lord gave you? Joy in praising with your whole heart.

#MoreJesusMoreJoy365WholeHeart

November

18

"Jesus said, 'I am the door, anyone who enters through me will be saved.'" (John 10:9, emphasis mine)

Today, let's envision what the door to heaven looks like. Jesus is the Judge standing at the narrow door, waiting to receive us with His strong arms. Share your vision in picture or words. Joy in the Door.

#MoreJesusMoreJoy365TheDoor

November

19

"God has united you with Christ Jesus. For our benefit God made him to be wisdom itself. Christ made us right with God; he made us pure and holy, and he freed us from sin." (1 Corinthians 1:30)

Today, let's celebrate our recovery from sin's hold on us. Jesus made us right with God and freed us from our sins. Let's thank Jesus for a changed heart and fly our freedom flags. What does your flag, "Live Free In Christ," look like to you? Joy in being freed from sin.

#MoreJesusMoreJoy365RecoveringSinner

November

20

"God decided in advance to adopt us into his own family by bringing us to himself through Jesus Christ. This is what he wanted to do, and it gave him great pleasure." (Ephesians 1:5)

Today, let's celebrate our adoption by Christ and our position as His children in His family of believers. Can you even count all the new family members that God gave you through Jesus? Which member will you always remember? Joy in being adopted by Christ.

#MoreJesusMoreJoy365AdoptedByChrist

November 21

"God saved you by his grace when you believed. And you can't take credit for this; it is a gift from God." (Ephesians 2:8)

Today, let's celebrate our salvation with praise, joy, and thanksgiving to Jesus. Through grace—the unearned love of God—we have been saved, i.e., rescued from our sin by our faith in Jesus. How do you celebrate the gift of grace you were given? Joy in our salvation.

#MoreJesusMoreJoy365SavedByGrace

November 22

"There is more than enough room in my Father's home. If this were not so, would I have told you that I am going to prepare a place for you? When everything is ready, I will come and get you, so that you will always be with me where I am." (John 14:2, 3)

Today, let's daydream about *the place* Jesus is preparing for us. What do you think that place will look like? Clouds above or below? Describe your beautiful image of *the place*. Joy in the Father's house.

#MoreJesusMoreJoy365MyFathersHouse

November

23

"Every time I think of you, I give thanks to my God." (Philippians 1:3)

Today, tell us for whom you thank God every time you think of them. Is it so awesome that we can praise God for everything and everyone who brings joy to our hearts. Maybe it's the gratitude that you hold in your heart for your pets. It is an honor and a blessing for us to praise God and thank Him for the ones He's put in our lives. Joy in being thankful.

#MoreJesusMoreJoy365thankful

November

24

"Epaphras, who is one of you and a servant of Christ Jesus, sends greetings. He is always wrestling in prayer for you, that you may stand firm in all the will of God, mature and fully assured." (Colossians 4:12, NIV)

Today, let's look at prayer. How and when do you pray for others? Do you stop what you're doing and pray when someone asks for prayer? We can wrestle in prayer on another's behalf anytime and anywhere. Joy in praying for others.

#MoreJesusMoreJoy365PrayersForOthers

November 25

"And Nehemiah continued, 'Go and celebrate with a feast of rich foods and sweet drinks, and share gifts of food with people who have nothing prepared. This is a sacred day before our Lord. Don't be dejected and sad, for the joy of the LORD is your strength!'" (Nehemiah 8:10)

Today, let's look at the joy God so freely gives us. Joy is God's gift to us. That gift can come in the form of strength. Having a thankful heart and attitude creates much joy. What is your definition of joy? How do you receive the joy He alone can give? Joy in the gift of His strength.

#MoreJesusMoreJoy365strength

November 26

"Enter his gates with thanksgiving; go into his courts with praise. Give thanks to him and praise his name." (Psalm 100:4)

Today, let's consider our attitude of gratitude when we enter church. Thanksgiving is the very beginning of worship. When we are full of thanksgiving, it is easy to praise His name. Try keeping a gratitude journal or do a bulletin board. What are some other ways we could cultivate gratitude? Joy in hearts of thanksgiving.

#MoreJesusMoreJoy365thanksgiving

November

27

"But watch out! Be careful never to forget what you yourself have seen. Do not let these memories escape from your mind as long as you live! And be sure to pass them on to your children and grandchildren." (Deuteronomy 4:9)

Today, let's share the lessons or miracles you've witnessed from Jesus. What has He taught you or let you see? When we talk about God and work Him into our conversations, we will never forget who He is and what He has done in our lives. Including Him helps others—especially the next generation—remember and know who Jesus is. Talking about God also cultivates gratitude in the heart of the one sharing. Joy in sharing who Jesus is.

#MoreJesusMoreJoy365NeverForgetJesus

November

28

"Shout with joy to the LORD, all the earth!" (Psalm 100:1)

Today, let's joyfully shout one word of praise to the Lord for all of the earth to hear. What is the one word you would shout? Would it be *forgiven, loved, peace, joyful,* or simply *thanks*? Joy in shouts to the Lord.

#MoreJesusMoreJoy365ShoutToTheLord

November

29

"For all these forty years your clothes didn't wear out, and your feet didn't blister or swell." (Deuteronomy 8:4)

Today, let's be reminded to thank God for the everyday things. Just like the Israelites, we too often forget to thank God for all that He has blessed us with. Thank Him for the mundane things that you use every day, like your car, appliances, electronics, and yes, of course, clothing. He usually only hears from us when one of our belongings breaks down, but let's remember to thank Him for everything. What's your favorite mundane blessing? Joy in the mundane.

#MoreJesusMoreJoy365MundaneJoys

November

30

"Has the LORD redeemed you? Then speak out! Tell others he has redeemed you from your enemies." (Psalm 107:2)

Today, let's tell our story with only using one line. Here it is; fill in the blank: "Jesus redeemed me from____." Declare God's goodness by what He has already done. Joy in being redeemed.

#MoreJesusMoreJoy365IAmRedeemed

December 1

"In those days Israel had no king; all the people did whatever seemed right in their own eyes." (Judges 21:25)

Today, let's remember that those days seem familiar these days, except we do have a King. Those who follow Jesus do as the King sees fit and answer to Him. We understand our worldview is different than that of the majority, but we stand firm in the truth of God and follow the rules He's given us. What is one of the rules that you follow daily that stands out? Joy in having a King.

#MoreJesusMoreJoy365TheKing

December 2

"But consider the joy of those corrected by God! Do not despise the discipline of the Almighty when you sin." (Job 5:17)

Today, let's consider it joy to be corrected by God. Although it usually doesn't feel joyful at the time, we can later see how and why God has corrected us. It is important and needful for the Father to correct His child when they sin. Discipline shapes us and helps us grow. In what area is God shaping you? Joy in being shaped by God.

#MoreJesusMoreJoy365ShapedByGod

December

3

"For to me, living means living for Christ, and dying is even better." (Philippians 1:21)

Today, let's consider Paul's words. To him, *to live* means "to live for Christ, spreading His word and telling others about Him." *To die is gain* means that we will see Jesus face to face, and all our worldly concerns will be gone. No more sorrows or pains. Really living means you are ready to die, at peace with it, even anticipating the day as Jesus' death and resurrection negated death's sting and gave us eternal life after physical death. Do you believe that *living* means "living for Christ"? Joy in living for Him now and seeing Him later.

#MoreJesusMoreJoy365NowAndLater

December

4

"And whatever you do or say, do it as a representative of the Lord Jesus, giving thanks through him to God the Father." (Colossians 3:17)

Today, let's be reminded that we represent Jesus all of the time, not just for an hour on Sunday. Others can see who Jesus is through us. What changes do we need to make in our life to better represent Jesus? Joy in being a representative of Jesus.

#MoreJesusMoreJoy365RepresentJesus

December
5

"But Jesus told him, 'No! The Scriptures say,
"People do not live by bread alone, but by every
word that comes from the mouth of God."
(Matthew 4:4)

Today, let's consider what your tank is running on. Is it every indulgent food you desire or is it being satisfied with the Word of God? What's in your tank? Let's recognize that we need God's Word daily in our life to satisfy our longings for other things. The Word points our love and desires back to Jesus. We need to obey the Word through practice and reading. Joy in not living on bread alone.

#MoreJesusMoreJoy365NotByBreadAlone

December
6

"There is salvation in no one else! God has
given no other name under heaven by which we
must be saved." (Acts 4:12)

Today, let's think of all the wonderful names of our God and write them down. Just start writing *Abba, Papa, Daddy, Bread of Life,* and when you get to your favorite, share it. Joy in the salvation of His name.

#MoreJesusMoreJoy365HisName

December 7

"I am the Alpha and the Omega—the beginning and the end," says the Lord God. "I am the one who is, who always was, and who is still to come—the Almighty One." (Revelation 1:8)

Today, let's begin and end our day with thanking God in prayer. We can thank Him for the great joy in the beginning of His creation, the joy we have today, and the anticipation and great joy in the ending that will come. What does your prayer of praise sound like today? Joy then, now, and to come.

#MoreJesusMoreJoy365JoyAlways

December 8

"All I have is yours, and all you have is mine. And glory has come to me through them." (John 17:10, NIV)

Today, let's give it all to Jesus. Everything is already His, and we are simply keepers of all that He has given us while we are here. What are you holding back from Him? Maybe it's a hurt, a pain or tithing. Whatever you're hanging on to…give it over to Him. Joy in giving it all.

#MoreJesusMoreJoy365GiveItAll

December 9

"And David danced before the LORD with all his might, wearing a priestly garment." (2 Samuel 6:14)

Today, let's praise the Lord with all our might! About what have you been so excited to praise God that you did it with all your might? Maybe you were dancing wholeheartedly before Him, completely speechless. Joy in praising Jesus with all our might!

#MoreJesusMoreJoy365PraiseJesus

December 10

"A voice of one calling: 'In the wilderness prepare the way for the LORD; make straight in the desert a highway for our God.'" (Isaiah 40:3, NIV)

Today, let's make straight paths for the Lord. Maybe this means digging out the curve in our own paths or maybe it's sharing who Jesus is with others. Whatever He places on your heart, move with it. Share with us as you are led. Joy in preparing the way for the Lord.

#MoreJesusMoreJoy365PrepareTheWay

December

11

"The Lord is my light and my salvation—so why should I be afraid? The LORD is my fortress, protecting me from danger, so why should I tremble?" (Psalm 27:1)

Today, let's remember that we are protected by God; we are His! We have no one and nothing to fear. What is your favorite scripture about God's protection? The next time you're afraid or worried, pull out this scripture and pray it out loud. Joy in His protection.

#MoreJesusMoreJoy365HisProtection

December

12

"My health may fail, and my spirit may grow weak, but God remains the strength of my heart; he is mine forever." (Psalm 73:26)

Today, find peace in the psalm of Asaph who reminds us that when we grow weak and start to fail, we will still be with the Lord forever. He will be our strength when times are hard. Do you know someone who could use this truth today? How will you share it? Joy in forever with the Lord.

#MoreJesusMoreJoy365forever

December

13

"The LORD is close to the brokenhearted; he rescues those whose spirits are crushed." (Psalm 34:18)

Today, let's think back to a time when your heart was broken and your spirit was crushed. Could you feel the presence of God being close to you? How did He pull you through this time? What a comfort it is just knowing this scripture and how He cares for us. Joy in God's comfort.

#MoreJesusMoreJoy365GodsComfort

December

14

"The LORD directs the steps of the godly. He delights in every detail of their lives. Though they stumble, they will never fall, for the LORD holds them by the hand." (Psalm 37:23, 24)

Today, let's spend some time with God and ask Him where to step next. With God's guidance, we will not fall. Where are your next steps? Joy in the Lord's delight.

#MoreJesusMoreJoy365LordsDelight

December

15

"Teach us to number our days, that we may gain a heart of wisdom." (Psalm 90:12, NIV)

Today, let's not have another day slip past us without starting a plan to complete what God has asked us to do. In prayer, ask for his guidance and wisdom to move forward. Take the first step today. Toward what are you taking that step? Joy in fleeting days.

#MoreJesusMoreJoy365NumberOurDays

December

16

"Worship the LORD with gladness. Come before him, singing with joy." (Psalm 100:2)

Today, let's share our all-time favorite praise and worship song. Is an old-fashioned hymn that takes you back to simpler days, or is it a full-on rock-out guitar riff? Let's sing our favorite song to Him with joy in our hearts. Joy in worship.

#MoreJesusMoreJoy365WorshipMusic

December

17

"Shout with joy to the LORD, all the earth!"
(Psalm 100:1)

Today, let's express our joy to the Lord. Join in as we shout our joyful praises to Jesus. What does joy look like to you? What does it sound and feel like? Joy in expressing it.

#MoreJesusMoreJoy365ShoutWithJoy

December

18

"He has removed our sins as far from us as the east is from the west." (Psalm 103:12)

Today, let's show exactly how far the east is from the west. What does sin's removal look like to you? Maybe it's an emotion or a geographic sign. As far as the east is from the west seems like an impossible distance. They never touch each other—exactly like our sin has been removed from us and can no longer touch us! Joy in the distance between the east and the west.

#MoreJesusMoreJoy365EastFromWest

December 19

"So his master said, 'Go out into the country lanes and behind the hedges and urge anyone you find to come, so that the house will be full.'" (Luke 14:23)

Today, let's consider ways to invite others to church. The Lord wants a full house, and He wants everybody to receive an invitation to meet Him. Who do you know that you can invite into the house of the Lord? What are ways we can invite others to church or to a church function? Joy in a full house.

#MoreJesusMoreJoy365FullHouse

December 20

"The virgin will conceive a child! She will give birth to a son, and they will call him Immanuel, which means 'God is with us.'" (Matthew 1:23)

Today, let's remind someone that God is with him or her. Write out Matthew 1:23 and pass it along. Just knowing that He is always with us brings such comfort. *Immanuel* means "God with us," and *Jesus* means "the Lord saves. God the Father wanted to make sure we knew that He sent His only Son, whose purpose is to be with us and save us. Joy in Jesus name.

#MoreJesusMoreJoy365Immanuel

December

21

"Father to the fatherless, defender of widows—this is God, whose dwelling is holy." (Psalm 68:5)

Today, let's remember that Jesus is always with us, and especially with those who are lonely. When you feel like no one cares, remember that your heavenly Father does. He loves us right where we are and invites us to come to Him. Share this with someone today. Joy in never being alone.

#MoreJesusMoreJoy365NotAlone

December

22

"And I am convinced that nothing can ever separate us from God's love. Neither death nor life, neither angels nor demons, neither our fears for today nor our worries about tomorrow—not even the powers of hell can separate us from God's love." (Romans 8:38)

Today, let's share this truth or another powerful truth of God. This compelling scripture is full of God's forever love that can never be taken from us. What is the most powerful scripture that you have ever read? How do you use that passage as your source of strength? Joy in forever loved.

#MoreJesusMoreJoy365ForeverLoved

December

23

"For the LORD your God is living among you. He is a mighty savior. He will take delight in you with gladness. With his love, he will calm all your fears. He will rejoice over you with joyful songs." (Zephaniah 3:17)

Today, we are reminded through the prophet Zephaniah to remain close to God who is our source of true happiness. How do you stay close to God? Through Him we have real joy, and He rejoices with over us with song. The Lord is our constant provider and source of joy. He saves us, loves us, takes away our fears and fills us with His joy and gladness. Joy in a mighty Savior.

#MoreJesusMoreJoy365MightyToSave

December

24

"Christ is the visible image of the invisible God. He existed before anything was created and is supreme over all creation." (Colossians 1:15)

Today, let's celebrate the anticipation of the birth of Jesus Christ with a sweet "Happy Birthday" song. Ask others to join in at your church Christmas Eve service. How did you sing to the King? Joy sent to us from the invisible God. Joy in singing to the King.   #MoreJesusMoreJoy365SingToTheKing

December 25

"She gave birth to her firstborn son. She wrapped him snugly in strips of cloth and laid him in a manger, because there was no lodging available for them." (Luke 2:7)

Today, let's celebrate Jesus' birthday. Even though the innkeeper had no room for Him, let's show Him that we do. Let's bake a special cake just to honor Jesus on His birthday. Show us your candles and celebration cakes. Joy in His birth.

#MoreJesusMoreJoy365HappyBirthdayJesus

December 26

"The Word became flesh and made his dwelling among us. We have seen his glory, the glory of the one and only Son, who came from the Father, full of grace and truth." (John 1:14, NIV)

Today, let's recognize where Jesus dwells among us. When we believe wholeheartedly in Jesus, a place is made just for Him. Is He welcome in our homes, our hearts, our workplace? Joy in His dwelling.

#MoreJesusMoreJoy365DwellsAmongUs

December

27

"For where two or three gather together as my followers, I am there among them." (Matthew 18:20)

Today, let's look at the Holy Spirit, who is God with us. Jesus is with us because we believers have the Holy Spirit living in us. He is with us through the Spirit, He hears our prayers, and when we seek and invite Him, He joins us in our time spent together in community. Share a time when you gathered with other believers and so did the Lord. Joy in the Holy Spirit.

#MoreJesusMoreJoy365GodWithUs

December

28

"Let me hear of your unfailing love each morning, for I am trusting you. Show me where to walk, for I give myself to you." (Psalm 143:8)

Today, let's be reminded that each morning is a new day to seek His Word and ask for His direction. Renew yourself each day, promising the Lord that you belong to Him. Let's write out a prayer of our steadfast daily faithfulness to Him. Joy in daily renewals.

#MoreJesusMoreJoy365DailyRenewal

December

29

*"Let love and faithfulness never leave you; bind
them around your neck, write them on the tablet
of your heart."* (Proverbs 3:3, NIV)

Today, let's write out the words *love* and *faithfulness* to help us remember to carry these characteristics into our daily lives. Love and faithfulness are the foundation for a good relationship. How do you show love and faithfulness to God, to your spouse, children, and to your friends? Joy in being loving and faithful to others.

#MoreJesusMoreJoy365LoveAndFaithfulness

December

30

*"And all nations will hate you because you are
my followers. But everyone who endures to the
end will be saved."* (Matthew 10:22)

Today, let's celebrate being a risk taker. Following Jesus is a risk; you may lose your family, your friends, and your life as you know it, but you'll gain everything. What have you most gained from following Jesus? Joy in risking it all.

#MoreJesusMoreJoy365RiskItAll

"The grass withers and the flowers fade, but the word of our God stands forever." (Isaiah 40:8)

Today, let's grab our Bible and carry it with us wherever we go. Are you working from home? Carry it with you throughout the house. Take it to work, gym, put it in your locker. Carry it with you in your hands and in your heart. Share your pictures. Joy in the Word.

#MoreJesusMoreJoy365JoyInTheWord

JOY

JESUS FREAK

~About the Author~

Sandy Holly and her husband James live in the cheese laden Midwest. Sandy has bachelor degrees in business and psychology, worked in non-profits, served on non-profit boards of directors, and volunteered for many different organizations. She has combined her life experience, chance encounter and relationship with Jesus, her passion for writing and encouraging others, and her creative need to "wear the Bible" to profess her faith to launch *Jesus Freak Apparel*. This is a one-stop-online shop for Good News clothing, accessories, and literature.

Sandy is passionate about reading, studying, and proclaiming the Word of God, and that is why *Jesus Freak Apparel,* is a proud supporter of Compassion International and Klove Christian radio. Compassion International releases children from poverty around the world in Jesus' name. Klove provides positive and encouraging stories from other Christians and inspiring music through Christian radio, which is broadcast around the world for all to hear about Jesus. Ten percent of every purchase is passed along to these organizations. To learn more, please visit Sandy's online store at JesusFreakApparel.com and learn how your purchase promotes the Good News for all to hear.

JesusFreakApparel.com

Read about Sandy's Testimony

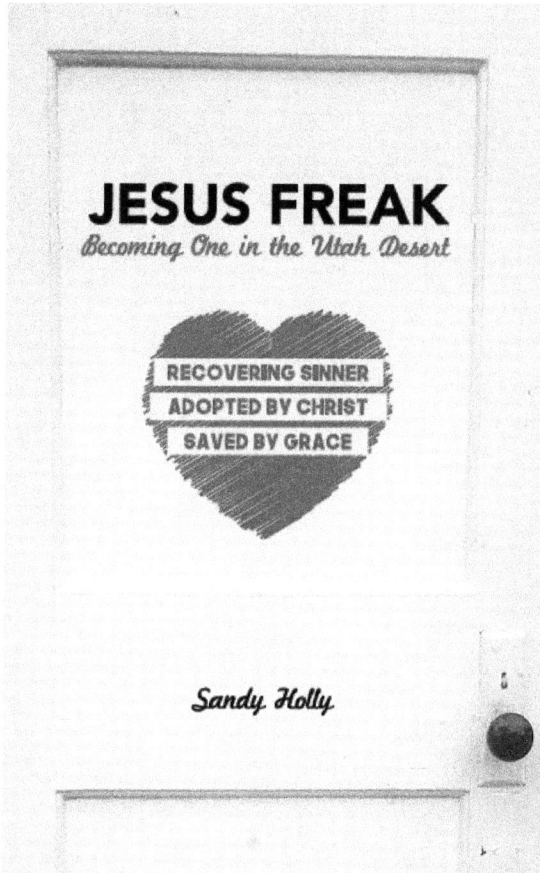

Come on an encouraging adventure in the middle of the Utah desert where God took away my complacent heart, and replaced it with a new compassionate one. This book came about as I began journaling through my Utah experiences of living and loving God in a place where it appeared others didn't. I was living in a paradox among the Mormons. I experienced a culture unbeknownst to me as well as my quest to know and understand the saving love that is the Christ. This is my story of becoming a "Jesus freak."

Reading the Bible in a year has never been easier!

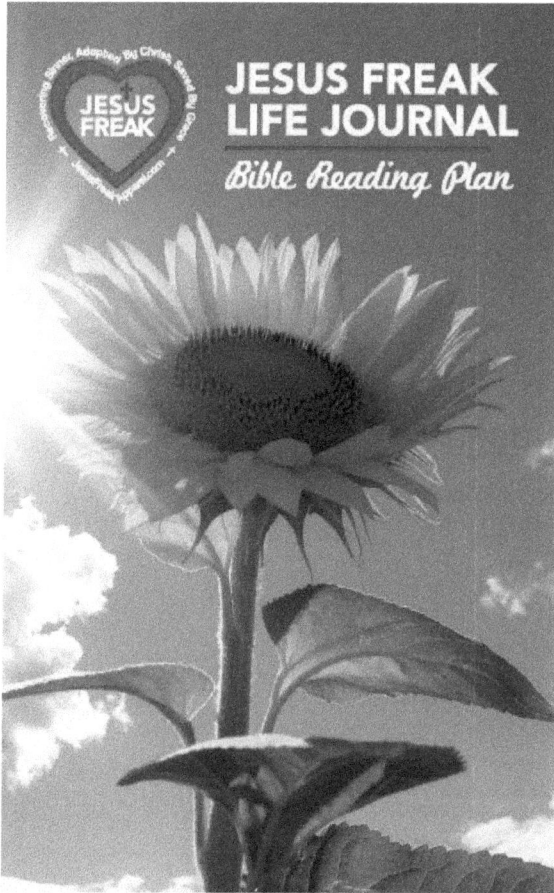

In just twenty minutes a day, you will read the Bible in a year! The *Jesus Freak Life Journal* Bible-reading plan combines readings from both the Old and New Testaments daily. Learn to journal your way through the Bible using the *SOAP* method of reading and applying Scriptures to your daily life. Available at JesusFreakApparel.com.

Yahoo! It's Time to Tell Your Story!
In your own Personal Journal available at
JesusFreakApparel.com

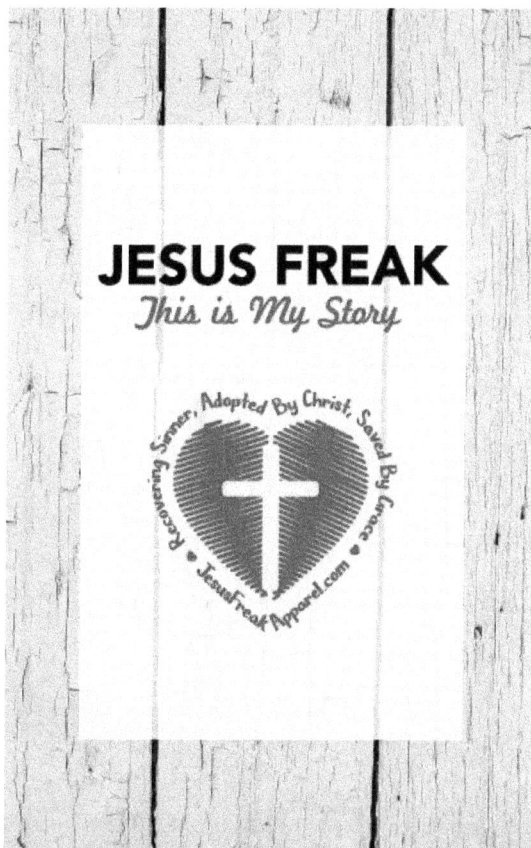

Everyone has a story to tell. May I encourage you to write your story and explore your life? Journaling your personal experience is a way of organizing your thoughts and helps you remember the character of God. You will find the places where God has shown up in the most beautiful ways. It was through journaling that God had the opportunity to grow and shape me. Will you let Him shape you?